Silk Knits

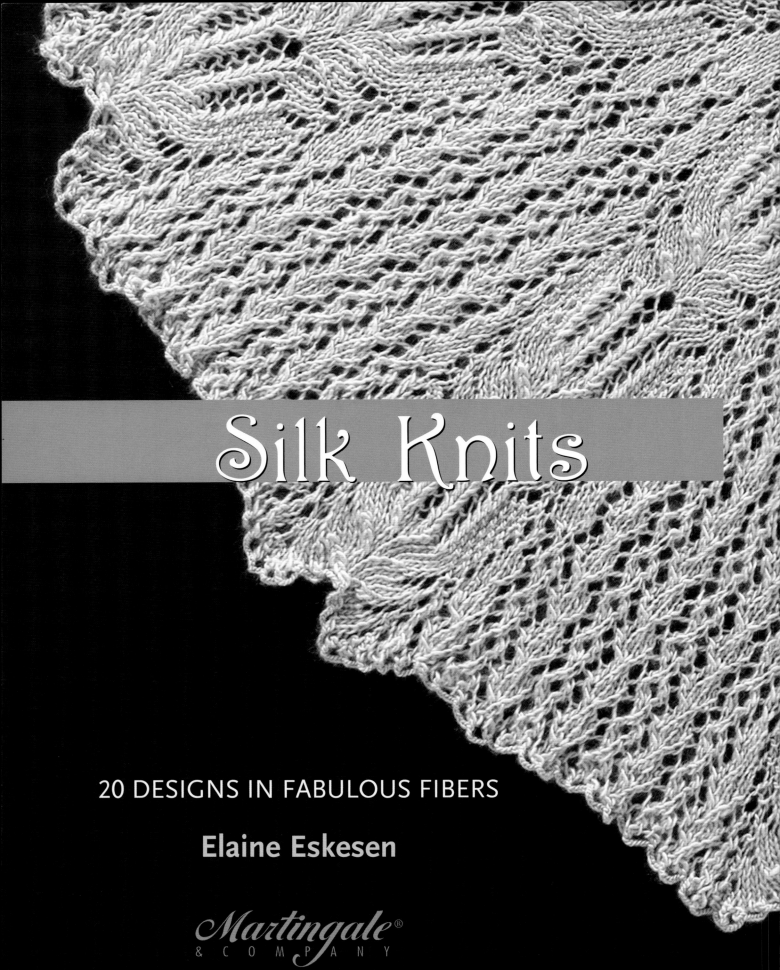

Silk Knits

20 DESIGNS IN FABULOUS FIBERS

Elaine Eskesen

Martingale®
& COMPANY

Silk Knits: 20 Designs in Fabulous Fibers
© 2007 by Elaine Eskesen

Martingale & Company
20205 144th Ave. NE
Woodinville, WA 98072-8478 USA
www.martingale-pub.com

Printed in China
12 11 10 09 08 07   8 7 6 5 4 3 2 1

Library of Congress Cataloging-in-Publication Data
Library of Congress Control Number: 2006020288

ISBN: 978-1-56477-690-7

MISSION STATEMENT

Dedicated to providing quality products
and service to inspire creativity.

CREDITS

President: Nancy J. Martin
CEO: Daniel J. Martin
COO: Tom Wierzbicki
Publisher: Jane Hamada
Editorial Director: Mary V. Green
Managing Editor: Tina Cook
Technical Editor: Ursula Reikes
Copy Editor: Liz McGehee
Design Director: Stan Green
Illustrator: Robin Strobel
Cover Designer: Stan Green
Text Designer: Constance Bollen, cbgraphics
Photographer: Brent Kane

Dedication

Mom Elaine, Grandma Eleine, and the author, Elaine Eskesen

To the Elaines in my life:
Eleine Chatillon Dunning (my grandma)
Elaine Dunning Eskesen (my mom)
Elaine MacLean (my dear friend)
For your shared visions and dreams as women

Acknowledgments

For keeping my store, Pine Tree Yarns, alive with good humor while I was writing patterns and designing garments, I thank my staff: Jane Griffin, Angela Dexter, and Sherry Hughes. In addition, my appreciation to Jane Griffin and Aloisia Pollock for knitting several of the projects, and to Angela Dexter for adding the finishing touches on several garments.

This book introduces four incredible designers whom I've had the good fortune to meet along the knitting path. Their love of the art of knitting shows clearly in the work they have produced for this book. Thanks to Aloisia Pollock for her Lace Shell and Houndstooth Pullover, Anne E Dill for her Frost Flowers Shawls, Laura Glazier for her Beaded Shrug, and Carla Giuffrida for her Circle Vest.

Incredible silk inspires incredible garments, and I happily created with silk from the following new yarn companies. Their generous support in giving me the silk yarn to make these projects, and their excitement in sharing their love of the fiber, allowed every stitch to be beautiful. Thank you Daphne at the Fibre Company, Jane at Jade Sapphire, Tracy at Tilli Tomas, Mimi at La Patrona, and Heike at Handspun on the Web.

Wonderful established yarn companies also shared their expertise in fiber and donated yarns for the projects. Thank you Kathy at Classic Elite Yarns, Annie at Himalaya Yarn, Jean at Cascade Yarns, Frederikka at Aurora Yarns, Jeannie at Fiesta Yarns, and Samira at Henry's Attic.

Thanks to Bev Lamoureux of Shipyard Glassworks, both for her flair in designing and for her generosity in donating the glass buttons to accentuate the beauty of the color and texture in the silk garments.

Again and again Mel Fuller, a fellow resident here in Damariscotta, has helped me figure out how to do things correctly when I was stumped by some area of the work in progress. Thanks, Mel, once again.

For the love of knitting and the creative process, I send my gratitude to everyone who has shared her passion with me.

Finally, as always, my love and appreciation to my supportive family, which includes my four children and my brother Hal, and to my circle of friends who understand the quiet world I need while doing my work. In particular, my daughter Emily did extensive work on the "About Silk: A Short History" section (page 12).

Contents

SPRING

SUMMER

FALL

WINTER

Preface

I've always been fascinated by silk. Perhaps this fascination is rooted in my childhood memory of a silk pillow, where my head would lie on sheer softness as someone read me a story. I've made clothes using fabulous silk crepes, with my grandma watching over me. She also taught me how to knit, although I don't remember knitting with silk as a child.

So now, with eager hands, I've taken to knitting with silk, exploring its many offerings of texture and color. I began to focus on silk when I started dyeing it in my studio. Silk takes dye well, and I'd eagerly put more kinds of silk and silk blends into the dye pot. Colors would emerge in this beautiful natural fiber that couldn't be obtained with any other fiber. Curiosity rules my life in some simple ways, and this fiber gained my immediate attention. I wanted to keep playing with it. The stitches, patterns, textures, and colors that one can create with silk are unique.

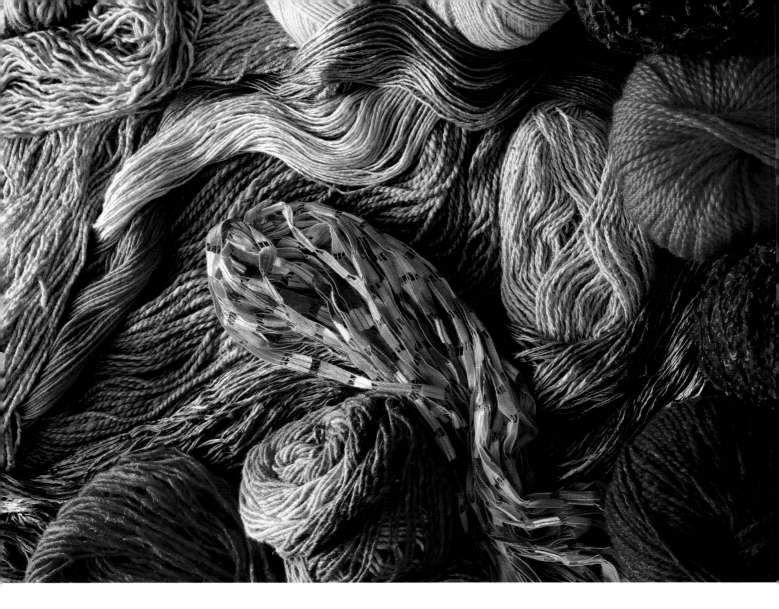

Why Choose Silk?

With the world of knitting opening its doors to fabulous yarns, it's time to concentrate on one fiber at a time. I want to start with silk. From the fiber to the finished product, we'll explore the elegant world of silk—its origin, beginning in China, its path along the Silk Road from Canton to Rome, and how the silkworm spread its cocoon through the East and the West.

Silk talks. It's the most lustrous of any natural fiber. It's delicate yet strong. It was described as the "woven wind" during Aristotle's time. Silk has durability, strength, elasticity, warmth, delicacy, and the ability to take color beautifully. (To learn how different kinds of silk and silk blends behave on the needle, refer to page 16.)

To talk about silk is one thing; to knit with it is quite another. This book focuses on patterns and knitted garments made with this luscious fiber. My fascination with silk will, hopefully, grab your attention as a knitter and spark your curiosity about the feel of the fiber. Since silk is so versatile, I've designed very different garments for many kinds of silk. Some of the silk I use has been blended with wool or alpaca to give it another exciting dimension.

My strength as a designer is in making garments that look great and feel good. The projects are easy to make, with simple instructions. I don't believe in complicated knitting, because we need a way to relax in the world today. I'll focus on the stitches, textures, and colors of the silk as it comes off the skein and becomes a knitted piece.

Find time each day to knit and explore the wonderful world of silk on your needles. I love silk, and sometimes I think I like touching the yarn more than actually knitting with it. I still have many silk hanks that will soon find a place on my knitting needles. What will I do with them? That's the question, and you'll have to wait and see.

Pure silk yarns

About Silk: A Short History

The Silk Road wasn't only a trade route for delivering the mysterious and elusive silk from the East into the waiting arms of the Western world; it was also a vital and phenomenally influential means to transfer knowledge, culture, and even religion. The name *Silk Road* itself is somewhat misleading, for it was by no means exclusive to silk goods and wasn't only one road, but a collection of routes that stretched over 8,000 kilometers—almost 5,000 miles—from east Asia to the Mediterranean. German geographer Ferdinand von Richthofen coined the name in 1877. In Chinese, the western portion of the Silk Road was called *Tian Shan nan Lu* or "the road south of the celestial mountains," and the eastern portion of the Silk Road (near Xi'an) was termed the *Imperial Highway.* It was originally composed of a number of caravan routes, dating from around 300 BC, along which jade was imported into China from the region around the central Asian town of Hotan. About 200 BC, these routes were extended to meet the Middle Eastern road system, and by 100 BC, this link became an active trade route between the Mediterranean world and China. At its height, the Silk Road's various routes ran from Xi'an, China, to the Mediterranean and Caspian shores, where trading boats often waited to carry the product farther.

The various branches of the Silk Road occupy some of the least hospitable terrain on the planet, the expanses that divide China from western Asia and Europe. These routes skirt the boundaries of a multitude of desolate and hostile regions, including the unforgiving Taklimakan Desert, or "Land of Death," as it's grimly referred to by locals. Here, sandstorms are a lurking threat to any traveler; rain is virtually unheard of—likewise vegetation—and temperatures can soar to 50° Celsius (122° Fahrenheit) and plummet to 20° below (-4° Fahrenheit). To the northeast lies the Gobi desert, equally unreceptive and treacherous, and below it sit the Himalaya, Karakorum, and Kunlun mountain ranges, whose few icy passes are dangerously narrow with heights of more than 5,000 meters (over 16,000 feet), with the odd precipitous drop into plunging ravines. And finally, to the north and west lie the Tianshan and Pamir ranges, respectively, which are significantly more welcoming but provide their own obstacles. To brave these conditions at the height of travel on the Silk Road, one had to have nerves of steel, an army of protection, a local to serve as guide, and a phenomenal product.

That phenomenal product, worth risking life and limb to buy or sell, was the silk, the star of the show on the various routes and in the trading townships. The Romans were first exposed to the lavish fabric around 50 BC from the Parthians who, they quickly decided, weren't nearly sophisticated and industrious enough to produce such a material. In quest of its source, the Romans may have learned from Parthian prisoners of the mysterious people in the East who produced such opulence, to whom they began referring as "the silk people," or *Seres.* When Roman society got a taste of the soft and luxurious material, silken goods exploded in popularity, causing both the Romans and the Parthians to send adventurous traders eastward in a fierce competition for the fabric. In only a few decades, all the ruling families of Rome were so anxious to attire themselves in silk that by 14 AD Emperor Tiberius, disgusted by the revealing bulges of this light and delicate fabric, forbade all men from wearing it. The mystery of silk's manufacture also captured the attention of society, riling Rome's intellectuals into a roaring fervor. While some affirmed that silk was obtained by "removing the down from the leaves with the help of water," others countered that it grew like wool in the forest. Once the intellectuals got involved, it became official: silk had made an irrevocable impact on the Western world.

Merchants didn't actually travel the length of the Silk Road. It's generally understood that very few people did—except a handful of diligent monks and the odd spy disguised as a missionary, sent from the West to discover the secrets of the East. Marco Polo is probably the most famous traveler on the Silk Road, voyaging from Venice to Beijing and back again in the late 13th century. Merchants and traders, on the other hand, would travel relatively short distances from each direction, acquiring goods at various points eastward and trading off those goods at points westward. The town of Os, about midway along the length of the Silk Road, was a popular meeting place for trade, and other small townships set up along the way flourished from the passing business. Because of the length and treacherous nature of the routes, silk and other products had long, drawn-out journeys and would be sold, resold, and traded, changing hands many times before reaching their ultimate destination.

The Silk Road played a similarly unique and central role in the processes of cross-cultural contact and exchange between Eastern and Western civilizations. Not only did goods move back and forth along its length, but technology, ideas, and culture did as well. It was a principal instrument in the spread of Buddhism from India to Central Asia and China, and Islam likewise arrived from the West along its hazardous precipices and desolate tracts. Ideas about mathematics, astronomy, and medicine traveled liberally east and west, along with different forms of music, dance, painting, and other arts. As far as goods were concerned, from China to the West passed not only silk, but jade, spices, ginger, tea, peach and pear trees, porcelain, papermaking, printing, and gunpowder. From the West into China came glass, grapes, cotton, wool, gems, ivory, and breeds of large horses. Because of the vast distances to be covered and the expense of transport, long-distance trade along the Silk Road was usually limited to items of high value and low bulk. Ideas, on the other hand, moved back and forth with much greater freedom, and religious word and spiritual laws could travel modestly in the hearts of monks.

Today, silk's mysteries are well known; we acknowledge that it doesn't grow in the forest or on the skin of leaves, but that it comes from the thread drawn off the silk-moth cocoon. We don't have to face barren deserts, icy cliffs, or ruthless bandits to wrap ourselves in soft luxury; silk is readily available in all styles and colors. The Silk Road, 4,000 years later, ends after spanning all the land and seas of the globe. It has passed the no-longer-elusive silk through hands, generations, and cultures and has successfully transported this precious commodity into every corner.

Swatching with Silks: A Designer's Exploration

The creamy colors and versatile textures of pure silk make every stitch a mystery until the fiber unfolds and becomes a swatch. Making a swatch from silk is like opening a fine bottle of wine; every sip, or in this case, stitch, is precious and celebrated.

The first thing I notice when looking at silk is its luscious appearance. How it looks and feels when holding it as a hank is generally how it'll feel while being knitted and how it'll look as a swatch.

There are many ways that silk can be spun or reeled, and that determines its appearance. Continuous long fibers reeled together give silk yarn a lustrous sheen. Shorter fibers, known as noils, aren't lustrous and look dull in comparison. The longer the fiber being spun, the stronger it'll be. Shorter fibers are weak and fragile. To test this, try breaking silk noil and see how easily it breaks compared to a single thread of spun silk used for embroidery. When working with silk, I always have my scissors handy as I can rarely break the yarn with my hands. A single strand of silk is stronger than any other natural fiber. When knitted, its strength can be a problem and if caught on something, a thread won't break but will snag and change the fabric's shape.

Feel the silk as you wind it into a ball; it's elastic. The give and stretching you have when knitting with silk is one of the many reasons to work with this fabulous fiber. Be aware that when it's knitted into a garment, it can lose its shape and stretch out. However, the fabric will come back when blocked. Since silk has a reputation for losing its shape, keep this in mind when knitting a garment. You might want to go down a needle size so the gauge is firmer. Making a garment a little shorter than if you were using wool will allow for some stretch as it grows.

Silk is extremely versatile; it's warm in winter and cool in summer. Whether it's fine or dense, it still shares these attributes. It can absorb moisture without feeling wet, more than other fibers, and therefore doesn't cling to the body. Silk is strong, yet fine; delicate, yet resilient; durable and long lasting. Garments made of the finest silk or those made of a heavier ply will be the warmest to wear in the winter and a good insulation to the cold outdoors. Yet the same fiber can be cool in the summer heat. So when swatching with silk, think seasons!

Whether you're making a swatch or a garment, there are some things you should know about caring for silk. It's probably best to put a skein of silk on a metal swift and wind it by hand. Silk's slipperiness can cause the silk yarn to fly off a skein winder before it's wound into a ball, leaving a mess on the floor. Care in winding silk is important.

When the ball is completed, care is also essential while knitting with silk. Silk is very strong, yet can be fragile. If your hands are rough from gardening, take the time to put on lotion before you sit down to knit. Silk will snag on anything, and your hands are a likely candidate.

Handle silk carefully. Keep it protected from everyday life. A silk project is not one I would choose to bring while watching my son at a hockey game. Silk can pill easily, so avoid a lot of handling or fussing with it. I keep the silk ball I'm knitting in a canvas bag to protect it from life's happenings.

I notice while knitting with 100% silk that my hands cramp up after an hour or so. Silk is slippery and it's easy to put more tension in the workings of those stitches, even without realizing it. So, I'll often shake my hands and stop knitting for a minute to get the tension out.

Blocking a silk swatch can be an adventure. I use a damp cloth, lay it on the garment or swatch, and press lightly with a hot iron to steam it. While blocking silk, I've noticed a disagreeable odor that reminds me of rotten fish. When I dye silk, it also has a rank smell when wet. This smell disappears when the silk is dry. However, if it gets damp or wet from rain or washing, the smell may reappear while it's wet.

I wash all my hand-knit things by hand, and silk is no exception. Soak your garment overnight in the sink with some liquid detergent. Don't agitate or move it around as this movement can cause pilling and allow the garment to stretch out. Before lifting out your garment, drain the sink and squeeze out excess water first. Silk is

extremely heavy when wet. Place the garment flat on a towel and carefully work it back into shape. Less movement is better for the life of your garment.

Storage of your garments is another matter. I have a cedar chest, which I treasure. I fold the sweater and place it loosely in the drawer. Don't hang a silk garment. It'll stretch out of proportion, and the hanger marks will appear on the shoulders and won't block out when pressed. I've ruined a beautiful sweater this way, so don't make this mistake. If you're concerned about pilling, you can put your silk sweater in a storage bag for extra protection.

Silk's versatility offers a full range of experiences, so try several types and see which type fits your specific knitting project or your personal knitting style. Following are some characteristics of 100% silk and a few blends in which silk and another fiber find a happy combination.

WORKING WITH 100% SILK

Different silks exhibit different characteristics. Knowing how different varieties behave can help you choose the right silk for a project.

Silk chenille. This silk doesn't slide well on the needle and, therefore, isn't fun to knit with.

I tried using metal needles to see if it was easier to work, to no avail. If you're a tight knitter, this isn't a good choice.

Muga wild silk. Crisp to the touch, this natural, wild silk is a pleasure to knit with. It has a nice crunch to it as I swatch and a lovely sheen while knitting.

Hand-spun silk. Fine threads to slubs show how versatile silk can be in the making and how strong the fiber is. It's hard to keep any tension as the silk sticks to the needle while knitting with it.

Silk noil. Course while running through your fingers, this feels more like cotton than silk. Not elastic when knitting with it, yet it does glide nicely on the needles. It's softer than other kinds of silk. It would make a nice summer bedspread.

Silk ribbon. Casting on with ribbon is hard because it doesn't have the give or elasticity of other silks. Ribbon has a hard time figuring out how to behave on the needles. It would be fabulous for a short-cropped summer shell.

Silk bouclé. Soft to the touch, silk bouclé is a sheer pleasure to knit with. It's light, yet dense; strong, yet has softness to its drape. The bouclé gives a bounce while knitting.

Two-ply tussah silk. Easy to knit, tussah silk has a wonderful feel and sheen. Its golden color perks up every stitch. It's firm yet soft to work with. Two-ply tussah silk would make a beautiful shawl.

Silk roving. This loosely spun silk presents a challenge if you're a gardener and have rough hands. Soft and pliable, this silk will give you a loosely knit fabric. It might be fun to use for a pillow cover

One-ply silk. If your stitches aren't even, it'll really show with this silk. It's beautiful when knit, but keeping an even tension while you're knitting is difficult. The challenge may be worth it, though, because this fiber shows how beautiful silk is.

WORKING WITH SILK BLENDS

Silk blends behave differently from all-silk yarns, and you have a number of options to choose from.

Silk and cotton. This blend allows the luster of silk and the substance of cotton to make a comfortable garment that'll have more memory and stay in shape. It feels nice to knit with; both fibers have a softness and smoothness that are a good weight for a summer project.

Silk and wool. The warmth of wool and the sheen of silk make this a dynamite combination. The additional attribute of wool being wrinkle-resistant allows this blend to be versatile in garment designs. I love knitting with this combination as the stitches have more loft than silk alone as well as luster and stability.

Silk and alpaca. The durability of alpaca along with its softness gives silk a smoother appearance while being knit. The blend has a nice bounce to it and is more giving than silk on its own.

Silk and linen. Linen is a plant fiber, and when blended with silk, it adds depth, body, and durability. When knitting with a silk-linen blend, I find I need to maintain careful control in order to keep the stitches even on every row. This blend produces beautiful, soft colors with little shine and would make a wonderful knitted fabric for any season.

Projects

SPRING

SUMMER

FALL

WINTER

Lace Shell

Lace Shell

Aloisia Pollock designed and knit this vest. This sturdy silk gives way to a lace pattern that happily shows each stitch. When knit, the silk-wool tweed blend produces unusual depth, texture, and color. The vivacious green looks like a spring day. Make it for the coming of warm weather.

Skill level: Advanced ◼◼◼▶

Sizes: X-Small (Small, Medium, Large)
Finished bust: 34 (36, 38, 40)"
Finished length: 20¾ (22¾, 24¼, 25¾)"

MATERIALS

4 (4, 4, 5) skeins of Silke-Tweed from
    Garnstudio (52% silk, 48% lamb's wool;
    50 g; 210 yds), color 21 (**3**)
Size 5 needles or size to obtain gauge
Stitch markers

GAUGE

24 sts and 32 rows = 4" in lace patterns

LACE PATTERN A

(Multiple of 19 sts)
Row 1 (RS): P4, K2tog, K3, YO, K1, YO, K3, ssk, P4.
Row 2 and all WS rows: Knit the knit sts and purl the purl sts as they face you, and purl the YOs.
Row 3: P3, K2tog, K3, YO, K3, YO, K3, ssk, P3.
Row 5: P2, K2tog, K3, YO, K5, YO, K3, ssk, P2.
Row 7: P1, K2tog, K3, YO, K7, YO, K3, ssk, P1.
Row 9: K2tog, K3, YO, K9, YO, K3, ssk.
Row 10: Knit the knit sts and purl the purl sts as they face you, and purl the YOs.
Rep rows 1–10 for patt.

LACE PATTERN B

(Multiple of 19 sts)
Row 1 (RS): P4, K2tog, K3, YO, K1, YO, K3, ssk, P4.
Row 2 and all WS rows: Knit the knit sts and purl the purl sts as they face you, and purl the YOs.
Row 3: P3, K2tog, K3, YO, K3, YO, K3, ssk, P3.
Row 5: P2, K2tog, K3, YO, K1, YO, sl 1, K2tog, psso, YO, K1, YO, K3, ssk, P2.

Row 7: P1, K2tog, K3, YO, K3, YO, K1, YO, K3, YO, K3, ssk, P1.
Row 9: K2tog, K4, YO, sl 1, K2tog, psso, YO, K3, YO, sl 1, K2tog, psso, YO, K4, ssk.
Row 10: Knit the knit sts and purl the purl sts as they face you, and purl the YOs.
Rep rows 1–10 for patt.

LACE PATTERN C

(Multiple of 22 sts)
Row 1 (RS): K2, YO, K3, ssk, P8, K2tog, K3, YO, K2.
Row 2 and all WS rows: Knit the knit sts and purl the purl sts as they face you, and purl the YOs.
Row 3: K3, YO, K3, ssk, P6, K2tog, K3, YO, K3.
Row 5: K4, YO, K3, ssk, P4, K2tog, K3, YO, K4.
Row 7: K5, YO, K3, ssk, P2, K2tog, K3, YO, K5.
Row 9: K6, YO, K3, ssk, K2tog, K3, YO, K6.
Row 10: Knit the knit sts and purl the purl sts as they face you, and purl the YOs.
Rep rows 1–10 for patt.

TIP: Knit the lace patterns once to practice them.

BACK AND FRONT

Work one back and one front the same.
CO 101 (107, 113, 119) sts.
(Knit 1 row, purl 1 row) 4 times; total of 8 rows.
Picot row: K1, (K2tog, YO) to last 2 sts, K2.
(Purl 1 row, knit 1 row) 4 (6, 8, 10) times; total of 8 (12, 16, 20) rows.
Knit 1 row on WS.
(Knit 1 row, purl 1 row) 4 (6, 8, 10) times; total of 8 (12, 16, 20) rows.

Eyelet row: K2, (K4tog, YO) to last 3 (1, 3, 3) sts, K3 (1, 3, 3).
WS of eyelet row: P3 (1, 3, 3), (K1, P1, K1 into YO, purl next st) to last 2 sts, P2.
(Knit 1 row, purl 1 row) 4 times; total of 8 rows.
Eyelet row: K3 (2, 3, 3), (YO, K4tog) to last 2 (1, 2, 2) sts, K2 (1, 2, 2).
WS of eyelet row: P2 (1, 2, 2), (K1, P1, K1 into YO, purl next st) to last 3 (2, 3, 3) sts, P3 (2, 3, 3).
(Knit 1 row, purl 1 row) 4 times; total of 8 rows.
Knit 1 row.
Picot row: K1, (K2tog, YO) to last 2 sts, K2.
Purl 1 row.
Beg lace patts, working RS and WS rows as follows:
RS rows: P3 (6, 9, 12), work lace patt 5 times, P3 (6, 9, 12).
WS rows: K3 (6, 9, 12), knit the knit sts, purl the purl sts, K3 (6, 9, 12).
Work lace patt as follows:
patt A twice (20 rows)
patt B once (10 rows)
patt A once (10 rows)
patt B once (10 rows)
patt A once (10 rows)
Shape armholes:
Row 1: BO 8 (11, 14, 17) sts, K4, YO, K3, ssk, P4, (row 1 of patt B) 3 times, P4, K2tog, K3, YO, K13 (16, 19, 22)—93 (96, 99, 102) sts.
Row 2: BO 8 (11, 14, 17) sts; knit the knit sts and purl the purl sts as they face you, and purl the YOs—85 sts for all sizes.
Row 3: Dec 1 st, K4, YO, K3, ssk, P3, (row 3 of patt B) 3 times, P3, K2tog, K3, YO, K6.

Lace Shell

Lace pattern A
(19 sts)

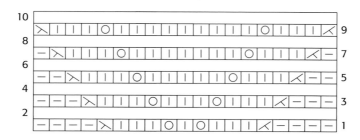

Lace pattern B
(19 sts)

Lace pattern C
(22 sts)

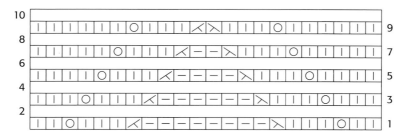

Key

⊡	Knit	⟋	K2tog
⊟	Purl	⟍	SSK
⊙	YO	△	sl 1, K2tog, psso

All WS rows: Knit the knit sts and purl the
purl sts as they face you, and purl the YOs.

Rows 4, 6, and 8: Dec 1 st; knit the knit sts and purl the purl sts as they face you, and purl the YOs—79 sts rem after row 8.

Row 5: Dec 1 st, K4, YO, K3, ssk, P2, (row 5 of patt B) 3 times, P2, K2tog, K3, YO, K6.

Row 7: Dec 1 st, K4, YO, K3, ssk, P1, (row 7 of patt B) 3 times, P1, K2tog, K3, YO, K6.

Row 9: K6, YO, K3, ssk, (row 9 of patt B) 3 times, K2tog, K3, YO, K6.

Rows 10, 12, 14, 16, and 18: Knit the knit sts and purl the purl sts as they face you, and purl the YOs.

Row 11: K2, YO, K3, ssk, P4, (row 1 of patt A) 3 times, P4, K2tog, K3, YO, K2.

Row 13: K3, YO, K3, ssk, P3, (row 3 of A) 3 times, P3, K2tog, K3, YO, K3.

Row 15: K4, YO, K3, ssk, P2, (row 5 of A) 3 times, P2, K2tog, K3, YO, K4.

Row 17: K5, YO, K3, ssk, P1, (row 7 of A) 3 times, P1, K2tog, K3, YO, K5.

Row 19: K6, YO, K3, ssk, (row 9 of A) 3 times, K2tog, K3, YO, K6.

Row 20: Knit the knit sts and purl the purl sts as they face you, and purl the YOs.

Rows 21–30: Rep rows 11–20 with lace patt B instead of A.

Shape neck: Knit row 1 of patt C over 22 sts, pm, K4, BO 27 (33, 39, 45) sts, K3, pm, knit row 1 of patt C. Working each side separately, BO 1 st on EOR at neck edge to marker, knit patt C over rem 22 sts. Knit patt C until armhole measures 8 (9, 9½, 10)". BO all sts.

FINISHING

Block pieces lightly. Sew side seams together. Sew shoulders together. Sew bottom edging under so that picot edge is at bottom.

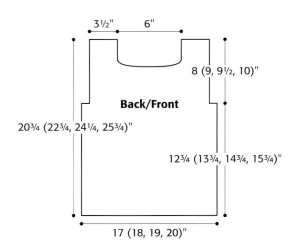

Shell with Sequins

Shell with Sequins

How fortunate to find beautiful, 100% silk to work with! Sequins give it additional luster and pizzazz, and I incorporated texture in the garment to take advantage of the sparkle. The delicate color illustrates how exquisitely silk can be dyed, while the simple shell silhouette keeps the focus on the yarn.

Skill level: Intermediate ◼◼◼▢

Sizes: X-Small (Small, Medium, Large)
Finished bust: 33 (35, 38, 40)"
Finished length: 18 (20, 20, 21)"

MATERIALS

4 (4, 5, 5) skeins of Disco Lights from Tilli Tomas (100% spun silk with sequins; 3.6 oz; 175 yds), color Nautical Blue ⓸
Size 5 circular needle, 16"
Size 7 needles or size to obtain gauge
Stitch holder
Stitch marker

GAUGE

20 sts and 26 rows = 4" in ripple st on larger needles

SEED STITCH

(Even number of sts)
Row/Rnd 1 (RS): (K1, P1) across.
Row/Rnd 2: (P1, K1) across.
Rep these 2 rows for patt.

RIPPLE STITCH

(Multiple of 6 + 5)
Row 1 (RS): K5, *P1, K5, rep from * to end of row.
Row 2: K1, *P3, K3, rep from * to last 4 sts, P3, K1.

26

Row 3: P2, *K1, P2, rep from * to end of row.

Row 4: P1, *K3, P3, rep from * to last 4 sts, K3, P1.

Row 5: K2, *P1, K5, rep from * to last 3 sts, P1, K2.

Row 6: Purl.

Rep these 6 rows for patt.

BACK

With larger needles, CO 83 (89, 95, 101) sts. Work in ripple st for 11 (12, 12, 12½)" or desired length to armhole.

Shape armholes: BO 6 sts at beg of next 2 rows—71 (77, 83, 89) sts. Beg seed-st band as follows: Work first 8 sts in seed st, work in established patt to last 8 sts, end with 8 sts of seed st. Dec 1 st at each armhole edge EOR 2 times—67 (73, 79, 85) sts. Cont with 6-st seed-st band at each armhole and established patt until armholes measure 7 (8, 8, 8½)". Put sts on holder.

FRONT

Work as for back until armholes measure 5".

Shape neck: Work 24 (26, 28, 30) sts, put 19 (21, 23, 25) sts on holder for neck, join second ball of yarn and work to end of row. Working both sides at same time, dec 1 st at each neck edge every row 3 times and EOR 3 times. Cont in established patt until armholes measure same as back.

FINISHING

Work 3-needle BO (see page 31) to join back and front at shoulders; leave back neck sts on needle.

Neckband: With smaller circular needle, PU sts around front neck, including front sts from holder, and back neck sts, so that you have an even number of sts, pm. Work 4 rnds of seed st. BO all sts.

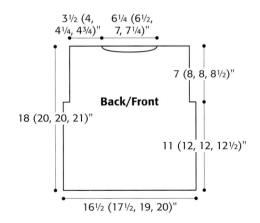

3½ (4, 4¼, 4¾)"   6¼ (6½, 7, 7¼)"

7 (8, 8, 8½)"

Back/Front

18 (20, 20, 21)"

11 (12, 12, 12½)"

16½ (17½, 19, 20)"

Rolled-Neck Cardigan

Rolled-Neck Cardigan

I've made this elegant rolled-neck cardigan several times with different types of yarn. This time, I chose a soft cotton-and-silk blend, uniting the softness and strength of the different fibers. Again, a simple stockinette stitch shows this fiber at its best. The V-neck shaping makes for a versatile garment; pair it with jeans for a casual look or wear dressy pants or a skirt for an evening at a nice restaurant. The yarn reminds me of a silk noil—firm and inelastic while it's being knit, then relaxed and comfortable when worn. I love the soft colors of this yarn and chose it for a summer sweater, although it could be worn in any season.

Skill level: Intermediate ◼◼◼◻

Sizes: X-Small (Small, Medium, Large, X-Large)
Finished bust: 32 (34, 38, 42, 46)"
Finished length: 22 (22, 23½, 25, 27)"

MATERIALS

9 (9, 10, 11, 11) skeins of Classic Silk from
  Classic Elite (50% cotton, 30% silk, 20%
  nylon; 50 g; 135 yds), color 6985 South Seas
  Coral ⓸
Size 5 straight needles and 36" circular needle
Size 7 straight needles and 36" circular needle
  or size to obtain gauge
Stitch holders
5 buttons, ⅞" diameter

GAUGE
18 sts and 22 rows = 4" in St st on larger needles

29

BODY

Cardigan is worked in the round up to the armholes, and then worked back and forth.

With smaller circular needle, CO 140 (148, 166, 184, 202) sts. Beg on RS, work in P3, K1 ribbing for 1". Change to larger circular needle and work in St st until piece measures 13 (13, 14, 15, 16)" or desired length to armhole, ending with a WS row.

Divide for front and back: K30 (32, 37, 41, 45) sts, BO 6 sts for underarm, knit to end of row. P30 (32, 37, 41, 45) sts, BO 6 sts for underarm, and work 68 (72, 80, 90, 100) sts for back. Put front sts on holders.

Back: Dec 1 st at each armhole edge EOR 4 times—60 (64, 72, 82, 92) sts. Work even until armhole measures 9 (9, 9½, 10, 11)". Put back sts on holder.

Fronts: Pick up sts from holder and dec 1 st at armhole edge EOR 4 times, AT SAME TIME, dec 1 st at neck edge every 4 rows 8 (8, 11, 13, 15) times—18 (20, 22, 24, 26) sts. Work until armhole measures same as back. Put shoulder sts on holder. Rep for second front.

SLEEVES

With smaller straight needles, CO 42 (42, 44, 46, 50) sts. Beg on RS, work in P3, K1 ribbing for 1". Change to larger straight needles and inc 4 sts evenly across row—46 (46, 48, 50, 54) sts. Work in St st, inc 1 st at each side every 4 rows 19 (19, 20, 22, 23) times—84 (84, 88, 94, 100) sts. Work even until sleeve measures 17 (17, 18, 19, 19)" or desired length. BO all sts.

FINISHING

Right front: With smaller straight needles, PU sts along edge until you reach the first dec for neck. Work in P3, K1 ribbing for 6 rows. BO all sts. Place buttons evenly spaced on band and sew in place.

Left front: With smaller straight needles, PU sts along edge until you reach the first dec for neck. Work in P3, K1 ribbing for 2 rows. **Row 3:** BO 2 sts for each buttonhole to correspond with button on button band and cont in P3, K1 ribbing. **Row 4:** CO 2 sts over BO sts. Work 2 more rows in P3, K1 ribbing. BO all sts.

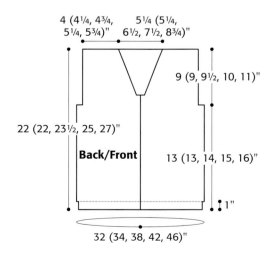

4 (4¼, 4¾, 5¼, 5¾)"   5¼ (5¼, 6½, 7½, 8¾)"

9 (9, 9½, 10, 11)"

22 (22, 23½, 25, 27)"

Back/Front   13 (13, 14, 15, 16)"

1"

32 (34, 38, 42, 46)"

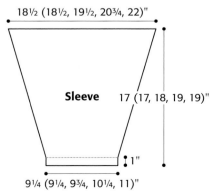

18½ (18½, 19½, 20¾, 22)"

Sleeve   17 (17, 18, 19, 19)"

1"

9¼ (9¼, 9¾, 10¼, 11)"

3-NEEDLE BO

Place front and back shoulder stitches onto 2 separate needles. Holding both needles in left hand with right sides of knitting together, use a third needle to knit together the first stitch from the front needle and the first stitch from the back needle. *Knit the next 2 stitches together, then bind off 1 stitch from right-hand needle. Repeat from * across row. When 1 stitch remains, cut yarn and pull through stitch to secure.

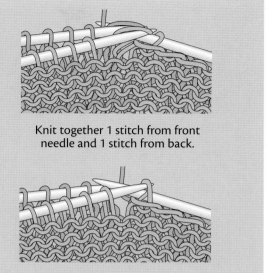

Knit together 1 stitch from front needle and 1 stitch from back.

Bind off.

Join fronts to back, using 3-needle BO (see above).

Rolled collar: With smaller circular needle, beg 1" from right-front band, PU sts along front neck; slip back neck sts from holder onto needle; PU sts along front neck, stopping 1" from left-front band. Work 10 rows of St st. BO all sts loosely. Tack under in a roll at beg and end of collar and at shoulders.

Eyelet-Yoke Pullover

Eyelet-Yoke Pullover

I put a skein of silk chenille with metallic thread into my hands and wanted to knit something simple and elegant. The nature of the yarn gives it a sophisticated look so I decided to make an eyelet-yoke sweater that'll dazzle any evening occasion. Chenille doesn't have a lot of give when knitting with it, so check your tension carefully. Tight knitters beware: you may be happier using metal needles to help the yarn glide easier on the needle.

Skill level: Intermediate ◼◼◼◻

Sizes: Small (Medium, Large, X-Large)
Finished bust: 34 (38, 40, 44)"

MATERIALS

8 (8, 9, 9) skeins of Silken Shimmer from Tilli
   Tomas (spun silk, silk chenille, and metallic
   thread; 3.5 oz; 150 yds), color Parchment
   (5)
Size 7 straight needles
Size 7 circular needles, 16" and 29"
Size 9 straight needles or size to obtain gauge
Size 9 circular needles, 16" and 29", or size to
   obtain gauge
Stitch markers

GAUGE

14 sts and 20 rows = 4" in St st on larger
   needles

SEED STITCH

(Even number of sts)
Rnd 1: (K1, P1) around.
Rnd 2: (P1, K1) around.
Rep rows 1 and 2 for patt.

BODY

Pullover is worked in the round up to the armholes. Work sleeves separately, then join sleeves to body and continue in the round for the yoke.

With smaller 29" circular needle, CO 120 (134, 140, 154) sts. Join and pm at beg of rnd. Work 4 rnds in seed st. Work eyelet patt as follows:

Rnd 1: Knit.

Rnd 2: Purl.

Rnds 3 and 4: Knit.

Rnd 5: *K2tog, YO, rep from * around.

Rnds 6 and 7: Knit.

Rnd 8: Purl.

Work 5 rnds in St st.

Work rnds 1–8 of eyelet patt once more.

Change to larger 29" circular needle and work in St st until body measures 14 (15, 15, 16)" or desired length to underarm.

Divide for front and back: At beg of row, BO 6 sts for underarm, K54 (61, 64, 71) sts for front, BO 6 sts, knit to end of rnd (back). Keep all sts on needle.

SLEEVES

With smaller straight needles, CO 34 (36, 38, 40) sts. Work seed st for 4 rows. Work eyelet patt back and forth as follows:

Rows 1–3: Knit.

Row 4: Purl.

Row 5: K1, *K2tog, YO, rep from * to last st, K1.

Row 6: Purl.

Rows 7 and 8: Knit.

Work 5 rows in St st.

Change to larger straight needles and work in St st, inc 1 st at each edge every 6 rows 7 (7, 8, 8) times—48 (50, 54, 56) sts. Work even until sleeve measures 16 (17, 17½, 17½)". BO 3 sts at beg of next 2 rows, keep rem sts on needle.

Join sleeves and body: With back body sts on needle, pm (use different color for this marker), put 42 (44, 48, 50) sleeve sts on needle, pm, work front sts, pm, put 42 (44, 48, 50) sleeve sts on needle, pm—192 (210, 224, 242) sts.

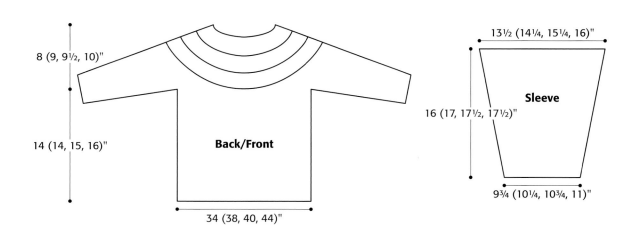

8 (9, 9½, 10)"

14 (14, 15, 16)"

Back/Front

34 (38, 40, 44)"

13½ (14¼, 15¼, 16)"

Sleeve

16 (17, 17½, 17½)"

9¾ (10¼, 10¾, 11)"

YOKE

At first marker (different-color one), beg yoke and dec as follows:

Rnd 1: *K1, sl 1, K1, psso, knit to 3 sts before marker, K2tog, K1, slm, rep from * 3 times—184 (202, 216, 234) sts.

Rnd 2: Knit.

Work last 2 rnds another 3 times—160 (178, 192, 210) sts after last dec.

Work even until 4½ (5, 5, 5)" from sleeve join.

Work eyelet patt in the rnd as follows:

Rnd 1: Knit.

Rnd 2: Purl.

Rnds 3 and 4: Knit.

Rnd 5: *K2tog, YO, rep from * around.

Rnds 6 and 7: Knit.

Rnd 8: Purl.

First dec rnd: *K2, K2tog, rep from * to last 0 (2, 0, 2) sts, K0 (2, 0, 2)—120 (134, 144, 158) sts.

Work rnds 1–8 of eyelet patt once.

Work 5 rnds in St st.

Second dec rnd: *K1, K2tog, rep from * to last 0 (2, 0, 2) sts, K0 (2, 0, 2)—80 (90, 96, 106) sts.

Work 3 rnds in St st; change to larger 16" needles when necessary.

Work rnds 1–8 of eyelet patt once.

Third dec rnd: *K1, K2tog, rep from * to last 2 (0, 0, 1) sts, K2 (0, 0, 1)—54 (60, 64, 71) sts.

Neck: Change to smaller 16" circular needle, work in seed st for 4 rnds. BO all sts loosely.

FINISHING

Sew sleeve seams and underarm seams.

Circle Vest

Circle Vest

Carla Giuffrida designed this wonderful Circle Vest. I was fascinated when she walked by my booth at Stitches East, and I asked the usual question: "How did you knit this?" So here is her pattern. I knit it in summer jewel colors, while Carla's version (on page 38) is in an earthy palette, so we each showed our individual flair. The vest is fun to knit. From experience, I promise you'll have lots of knitters wondering what you're doing while the vest is on the needles and in progress. The way the colors change while the circle gets bigger is fun to watch and will keep you knitting far into the night.

Skill level: Intermediate ◼◼◼◻

Sizes: Small (Medium, Large)
Finished bust: 36 (38, 40)"

MATERIALS

5 (6, 7) balls of Silk Garden from Noro (45% silk, 45% kid mohair, 10% lamb's wool; 50 g; 100 m), color 87 (④)
Size 9 dpn or size to obtain gauge
Size 9 circular needles, 16" and 29", or size to obtain gauge
Small amount of waste yarn
8 stitch markers
Optional: Decorative pin

GAUGE

14 sts and 20 rows = 4" in ribbing patt

Circle Vest

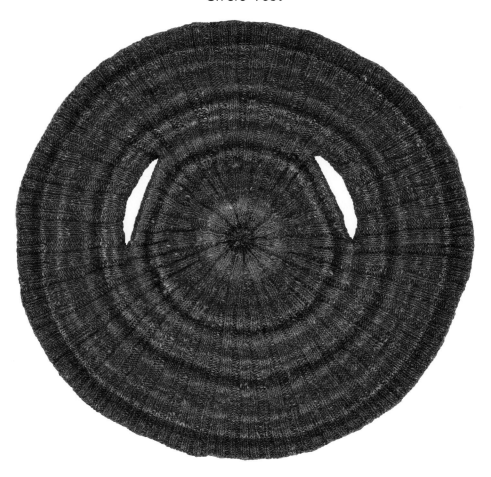

INCREASES

Inc 1 K st: With the yarn in back, insert the needle from front to back into the stitch below the next stitch on the needle and knit in the usual manner.

Inc 1 P st: With the yarn in front, insert the needle from back to front into the stitch below the next stitch on the needle and purl in the usual manner.

BODY

The vest is worked from the center out. Start with double-pointed needles and switch to 16" and 29" circular needles as needed.

CO 8 sts on 1 dpn.

Rnd 1: Knit in front and back of each st—16 sts. Divide sts onto 4 needles, join and pm.

Rnd 2: *K1, inc 1 K st, K1 (this is the stitch on the needle above the st you just knit), rep from * around—6 sts per needle.

Rnd 3: (K1, P1) around.

Rnd 4: *K1, inc 1 P st, P1 (this is the stitch on the needle above the st you just purled), rep from * around—9 sts per needle.

Rnd 5: (K1, P2) around.

Rnd 6: *Inc 1 K st, K1, P2, rep from * around. Change to 16" circular needle—12 sts per needle.

Rnd 7: (K2, P2) around, pm after every 6th st. Each needle now has 2 sections separated by a marker. Notice in which section the tail is because this is the first needle of the round.

NOTE: Continue on double-pointed needles until you can easily work on the 16" circular needle. When moving stitches from the double-pointed needles to the circular needle, keep the markers in place as established, and add 1 additional marker after the last stitch on each double-pointed needle. Use a different-colored marker for the beginning of the round. You should have 8 markers that divide the stitches into 8 sections.

Rnd 8: *K2, P2, K1, inc 1 K st, K1, slm, P2, K2, P1, inc 1 P st, P1, slm (if you're still on dpns, you don't have a marker to slip; move to next needle), rep from * around—7 sts in each section.

NOTE: The ribbing pattern is always growing from K1, P1 to K4, P4 as you continue to increase one stitch in each of the eight sections on even-numbered rounds throughout the vest.

Rnd 9 and all odd-numbered rnds: Knit the knit sts and purl the purl sts as they face you, keeping the ribbing patt as established.

Rnd 10: *K2, P2, K1, inc 1 K st, K2, slm, P2, K2, P1, inc 1 P st, P2, slm, rep from * around.

Rnd 12: *K2, P1, inc 1 P st, P1, K4, slm, P2, K1, inc 1 K st, K1, P4, slm, rep from * around.

Rnd 14: *K2, P1, inc 1 P st, P2, K4, slm, P2, K1, inc 1 K st, K2, P4, slm, rep from * around.

Rnd 16: *K1, inc 1 K st, K1, P4, K4, slm, P1, inc 1 P st, P1, K4, P4, slm, rep from * around.

Rnd 18: *K1, inc 1 K st, K2, P4, K4, slm, P1, inc 1 P st, P2, K4, P4, slm, rep from * around.

Now you'll start inc again to start a new set of ribs, starting as before with the farthest rib from each marker.

Rnd 20: *K4, P4, K2, inc 1 P st, K2, slm, P4, K4, P2, inc 1 K st, P2, slm, rep from * around.

Rnd 22: *K4, P4, K2, inc 1 P st, P1, K2, slm, P4, K4, P2, inc 1 K st, K1, P2, slm, rep from * around.

Rnd 24: *K4, P2, inc 1 K st, P2, K2, P2, K2, slm, P4, K2, inc 1 P st, K2, P2, K2, P2, slm, rep from * around.

Rnd 26: *K4, P2, inc 1 K st, K1, P2, K2, P2, K2, slm, P4, K2, inc 1 P st, P1, K2, P2, K2, P2, slm, rep from * around.

Rnd 28: *K2, inc 1 P st, K2, (P2, K2) 3 times, slm, P2, inc 1 K st, P2, (K2, P2) 3 times, slm, rep from * around.

Rnd 30: *K2, inc 1 P st, P1, K2, (P2, K2) 3 times, slm, P2, inc 1 K st, K1, P2, (K2, P2) 3 times, slm, rep from * around.

You now have K2, P2 established all the way around. You'll go back and inc 1 rib at a time in each section to 4 sts in the same manner, always placing the inc in the middle of each existing rib. In other words, start again with the same method used in rnd 8, except that you'll have more ribs to work across. Cont until piece measures 8¾ (9¼, 9¾)" from center to needles. This is one-half of 17½ (18½, 19½)", which is the armhole-to-armhole measurement across back. For a larger back, divide measurement in half and work to that number. For example, if your back measures 20" from armhole to armhole, work to 10" from center, and then shape armholes. On next odd-numbered rnd (a rnd without inc), beg armhole shaping.

Shape armholes: Beg at first marker, using waste yarn, work next 22 (26, 28) sts and drop waste yarn. Slip these sts back onto left needle. Work them again with the project yarn and then cont in patt over next 46 (50, 54) sts. Then use another piece of waste yarn to work next 22 (26, 28) sts. Drop waste yarn. Slip these sts back to left needle and cont with project yarn in patt to end of rnd. Work the next rnd as usual, making inc where necessary.

Cont with circle, inc as established, until piece measures 18 (19, 20)" from center to needles, or half of your actual bust measurement. BO all sts loosely.

FINISHING

Carefully pick out the waste yarn and work a row of slip-stitch crochet around armhole very loosely as you remove the waste yarn. Fasten off and weave in ends. Use tail from CO to gather up the CO sts and close the hole in the center.

To wear, fold shawl collar back over smaller section between armholes; place arms in holes. If you wish, bring the shawl collar around your neck and pin the front together at the bust, using a decorative pin.

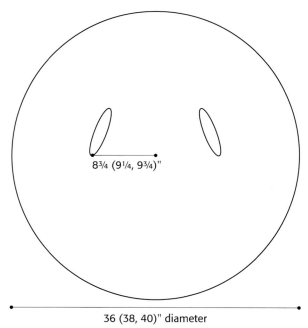

8¾ (9¼, 9¾)"

36 (38, 40)" diameter

Sicilian Pullover

Sicilian Pullover

I found my favorite summer pullover while living in Sicily, so naturally I wanted to make it up as a pattern. I used a pima cotton–and-silk blend, which has a natural sheen and abounds in rich color, and added a simple stitch pattern to exemplify the beauty of this yarn. It's a great sweater for a cool summer evening or while sitting in front of a fire during a snowstorm. This project shows me how versatile silk can be when wearing it. It's an all-season fiber, so I wear this sweater throughout the year.

Skill level: Intermediate ◖■■◻

Sizes: Small (Medium, Large, X-Large)
Finished bust: 34 (38, 42, 48)"
Finished length: 20 (21, 22, 24)"

MATERIALS

8 (8, 9, 10) skeins of Pima Silk from Cascade
   Yarns (85% cotton, 15% silk; 2 oz; 109 yds),
   color 5134 (4)
Size 5 needles
Size 7 needles or size to obtain gauge
Size E-4 (3.5 mm) crochet hook
Stitch holders

GAUGE

18 sts and 12 rows = 4" in St st on larger
   needles

PATTERN STITCH

(Multiple of 4 + 2)
Row 1 (RS): K1, *P1, K3, rep from * to
   last st, K1.
Row 2: Purl.
Row 3: Knit.
Row 4: Purl.
Row 5: K1, *K2, P1, K1, rep from * to
   last st, K1.
Row 6: Purl.

Row 7: Knit.

Row 8: Purl.

Rep rows 1–8 for patt.

BACK

With smaller needles, CO 78 (86, 98, 110) sts. Work in K1, P1 ribbing for 1". Change to larger needles, beg patt, and cont until piece measures 12 (13, 13, 14)" from beg.

Shape armholes: BO 8 sts at beg of next 2 rows—62 (70, 82, 94) sts. Work in established patt until armholes measure 8 (8, 9, 10)" or desired length. Put all sts on holder.

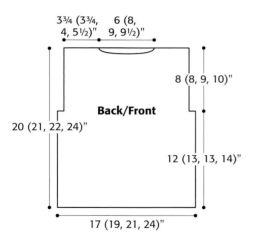

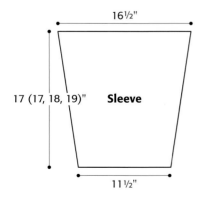

FRONT

Work as for back until armholes measure 5 (5, 6, 7)".

Shape neck: K22 (22, 26, 30), BO 18 (26, 30, 34) sts for neck, and work to end of row. Purl next row, adding a second ball of yarn at neck edge. Work both sides, dec 1 st at each neck edge EOR 5 times—17 (17, 21, 25) sts. Work until front measures same length as back. Put all sts on holders.

SLEEVES

With smaller needles, CO 52 sts. Work in K1, P1 ribbing for 1". Change to larger needles, beg patt, and inc 1 st at each edge every 6 rows 12 times. Work until sleeve measures 17 (17, 18, 19)". BO all sts.

FINISHING

Work 3-needle BO (see page 31) to join back and front at shoulders; BO back sts. Sew side seams. Sew sleeve seams. Sew in sleeves. With crochet hook, work 1 row sc around neck.

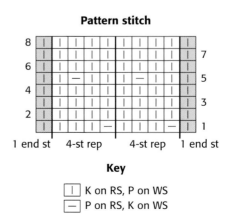

Pattern stitch

Key

☐ K on RS, P on WS
— P on RS, K on WS

Ribbon Vest

Ribbon Vest

Silk ribbon can be challenging, because it doesn't have a lot of give. Yet when knit, it drapes beautifully. This particular ribbon mesmerizes, each stitch changing to a new color. To show off the fun color combinations, I made an easy K2, P2 ribbed vest. Wear it alone or over a blouse.

Skill level: Beginner ◼☐☐☐

Sizes: Small (Medium, Large)
Finished bust: 34 (38, 42)"
Finished length: 20"

MATERIALS

5 (5, 6) skeins of Ischia Silk from Bollicine (Cascade Yarns) (64% silk, 32% cotton, 4% polyamide; 50 g; 71 yds), color 4003 (5)
Size 11 circular needle, 29", or size to obtain gauge
Stitch holders
Stitch markers

GAUGE

12 sts and 16 rows = 4" in ribbing patt

BODY

Vest is worked in the round up to the armholes, and then worked back and forth.

CO 100 (112, 124) sts and join into rnd, being careful not to twist sts, pm at beg of rnd. Work in K2, P2 ribbing for 11" or desired length to armhole.

Divide for front and back as follows: At beg of next rnd, BO 6 sts for left underarm, work in established ribbing for 44 (50, 56) sts (for front), BO 6 sts for right underarm, and work 44 (50, 56) sts in established ribbing to end of rnd (for back). Put front sts on a holder.

BACK

Cont in established ribbing, dec 1 st at each armhole edge EOR 2 times—40 (46, 52) sts. Work until armhole measures 9" or desired length and put sts on holder.

FRONT

Place 44 (50, 56) front sts onto needle and work as for back in established ribbing, dec 1 st at each armhole edge EOR 2 times—40 (46, 52) sts. When armhole measures 2", beg V-neck. Work 18 (21, 24) sts, K2tog, add second ball of yarn, K2tog, and work to end of row. Work both sides of V-neck in established ribbing, dec 1 st at each neck edge EOR until 10 sts rem on each side. Work even until each side of front measures same length as back.

FINISHING

Work 3-needle BO (see page 31) at shoulders; keep back neck sts on needle.

Neckband: Knit sts on back neck and PU sts around V-neck. Join, pm, and work 4 rnds in St st. BO all sts.

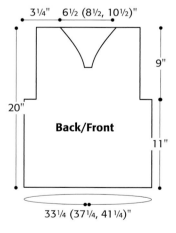

3¼" 6½ (8½, 10½)"

9"

20"

Back/Front

11"

33¼ (37¼, 41¼)"

Rib Shawl

Rib Shawl

Using a natural, two-ply silk, I wanted to emphasize how lustrous silk is as a natural fiber.

We knit for many reasons. My daughter, Robin, is getting married, and I designed and knitted this shawl for her to wear on this happiest of days. The coast of Maine in summer can bring a variety of circumstances, so this elegant shawl can measure up to natural surroundings during the evening festivities.

Skill level: Intermediate ◼◼◼◻

One size: 26" x 50"

MATERIALS

3 skeins of Spun Silk NM 4/2 from Henry's Attic (100% silk; 5 oz; 315 yds), color Crème

Size 5 needles or size to obtain gauge

Size E-4 (3.5 mm) crochet hook

GAUGE

24 sts and 26 rows = 4" in patt

PATTERN STITCH

(Multiple of 12 + 7)

Row 1 (RS): P1, *(K1, P1) 3 times, (K2tog, then knit first st again) 3 times, rep from * to last 6 sts, (K1, P1) 3 times.

Rows 2 and 4: Knit the knit sts and purl the purl sts as they face you.

Row 3: *(P1, K1) 4 times, (K2tog, then knit first st again) 2 times, rep from * to last 7 sts, (P1, K1) 3 times, P1.

Rep these 4 rows for patt.

DIRECTIONS

CO 156 sts. Work in patt st until shawl measures 50" or desired length. BO all sts.

Fringe: Cut enough strands of yarn, 14" long, to go along both short edges. We used 3 strands per fringe; use more if you want a thicker fringe. For each fringe, fold 3 strands at a time in half. Insert crochet hook into st along short end and draw folded fringe from the front to the back. Pull yarn through the loop and tighten. Cont evenly across edge. Rep for second short end. Trim fringe as needed.

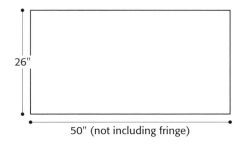

26"

50" (not including fringe)

Slip-Stitch Vest

Slip-Stitch Vest

I used rainbow-dyed silk for this elegant vest, and each stitch was a pleasure. The slip-stitch pattern breaks up the yarn's steady color sequence, allowing the hues to move around in the finished piece. For most silk yarns, a simple pattern is best. The silk wants, and deserves, all the attention.

Skill level: Intermediate ◼◼◼◻

Sizes: X-Small (Small, Medium, Large)
Finished bust: 32 (33½, 36, 40)"
Finished length: 20 (20, 21, 23)"

MATERIALS

3 (3, 4, 4) skeins of Fiesta La Luz (100% silk;
    2 oz; 210 yds), color 17125, Safari 🧶3
Size 4 circular needle, 16" and 29"
Size 6 circular needle, 29", or size to obtain
    gauge
Stitch holders
Stitch markers
8 glass buttons by Shipyard Point Glassworks,
    ⅜" diameter

GAUGE

20 sts and 28 rows = 4" in patt on larger
    needles

BODY

Vest is worked in the round up to the armholes, and then worked back and forth.

With smaller 29" circular needle, CO 160 (168, 180, 200) sts. Join into rnd and pm at beg of row. Work 2 rnds in K1, P1 ribbing. Work 4 rnds in P1, K1 ribbing. Rep these 6 rnds once more. Change to larger needle and beg patt st and front center panel.

Rnds 1 and 2: K37 (39, 42, 47) sts, pm for front band, (K1, P1) 3 times, pm, K37 (39, 42, 47) pm for side, knit to end of rnd.

Rnds 3 and 4: *K3, sl 1*, rep from * to * to marker, (P1, K1) 3 times, rep from * to * to end of rnd. (Knit any rem sts after working full patt reps.)

Rnds 5 and 6: Knit to marker, (P1, K1) 3 times, knit to end of rnd.

Rnds 7 and 8: K1, *sl 1, K3*, rep from * to * to marker, (P1, K1) 3 times, rep from * to * to end of rnd.

Cont working the 8 rnds for front center panel and slip-st patt until piece measures 11 (11, 12, 13)" or desired length to armhole.

Divide for front and back: Put 80 (84, 90, 100) sts on holder for front. On back sts, working back and forth in established sl-st patt (purling on WS rows), BO 3 sts at beg of next 2 rows. Dec 1 st at each armhole edge EOR 3 times—68 (72, 78, 88) sts. Work until armhole measures 9 (9, 9, 10)". Put all sts on holder.

Shape V-neck: Move front sts to needle. BO 3 sts at beg of next 2 rows. On next row, work to center panel, work 1 st, ssk, join 2nd ball of yarn, K2tog, work 1 st, then work to end of row. Working back and forth in established patt, dec 1 st at each armhole edge EOR 3 times and AT SAME TIME dec 1 st at each neck edge EOR until you have 20 (22, 22, 24) sts on each side. Work until fronts measure same length as back.

FINISHING

Work 3-needle BO (see page 31) to join back and front at shoulders, leaving back neck sts on holder.

V-neck: With smaller 16" needle, PU right front sts, left front sts, and back sts from holder. Work 2 rnds in K1, P1 ribbing. On next rnd, work P1, K1 ribbing to middle of front panel, sl 2 sts kw, K1, p2sso, cont in P1, K1 patt. Work 1 more rnd in P1, K1 ribbing. With larger needle, BO all sts.

Armbands: With 16" smaller needle, PU sts around armhole and work 2 rnds in K1, P1 ribbing. Work 2 rnds of P1, K1 ribbing. BO all sts.

Sew on buttons, evenly placing them on front panel.

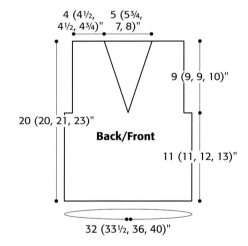

4 (4½, 4½, 4¾)" 5 (5¾, 7, 8)"

9 (9, 9, 10)"

20 (20, 21, 23)"

Back/Front

11 (11, 12, 13)"

32 (33½, 36, 40)"

Tab Pullover

Tab Pullover

Hand-spun yarn brings out all the mysteries of silk—its strength, its beautiful sheen, and the way the skein takes dye to make a fabulous color. In this Fibre Company merino, alpaca, and silk blend, we see how differently each natural fiber takes dye. I chose earth tones, but any color combination would be a winner in this simple design.

While knitting, you'll notice that the yarn moves gracefully from thick to thin, which is the nature of this particular hand-spun. Enjoy the magic. This pullover is knit in stockinette stitch to best display the silk's color and texture. The tabs and buttons give it flair and allow you to choose your own accent.

Skill level: Intermediate ◀■■▷

Sizes: X-Small (Small, Medium, Large, X-Large)
Finished bust: 36 (38, 40, 42, 44)"
Finished length: 24 (24, 25, 25, 25)"

MATERIALS

Terra from The Fibre Company (60% merino, 20% silk, 20% baby alpaca; 50 g; 100 yds)
（4）
  MC 6 (6, 6, 7, 7) skeins color Henna
  CC 3 (3, 3, 3, 4) skeins color Acorn
Size 6 straight needles and 16" circular needle
Size 8 needles or size to obtain gauge
Stitch holders
7 JHB coconut buttons, ⅝" diameter

GAUGE

16 sts and 20 rows = 4" in St st on larger needles

SEED STITCH

(Even number of sts)

Row 1: (K1, P1) to end.

Row 2: (P1, K1) to end.

Rep rows 1 and 2 for patt.

BACK

With smaller needles, CO 48 (50, 52, 56, 58) sts with MC and 24 (26, 28, 28, 30) sts with CC—72 (76, 80, 84, 88) total sts. On first row, beg seed-st band, joining 2 colors as shown below. Work in seed st for 1½". Change to larger needles and beg dovetail patt on RS as follows: K51 (53, 55, 59, 61) sts with MC and K21 (23, 25, 25, 27) sts with CC. Work in St st, following chart until body measures 16" from beg, ending with a WS row.

Shape armholes: BO 5 sts at beg of next 2 rows—62 (66, 70, 74, 78) sts. Cont in dovetail patt until piece measures 24 (24, 25, 25, 25)" from beg. Put all sts on holder.

LEFT FRONT

With smaller needles, CO 28 (30, 32, 32, 34) sts with CC. Work in seed st for 1½". Change to larger needles and work in St st for 20 (22, 24, 24, 26) sts. Cont to work 8 sts of seed st for left-front edge. Work until piece measures 16" from beg, ending with WS row.

Shape armhole: BO 5 sts at beg of next row—23 (25, 27, 27, 29) sts. Cont in established patt until armhole measures 6", ending with a WS row.

Shape neck: K6 and put these 6 sts on holder for neck opening. Dec 1 st at neck edge EOR 3 (3, 4, 4, 5) times—14 (16, 17, 17, 18) sts. Work until armhole measures same length as back. Put shoulder sts on holder.

RIGHT FRONT

With smaller needles, CO 52 (54, 56, 60, 62) sts with MC. Work in seed st for 1½", ending with WS row. Change to larger needles and

INTARSIA JOIN

To keep holes from appearing in the knitting when changing colors, the two yarns must be twisted around each other. Always pick up the new yarn underneath the yarn just worked.

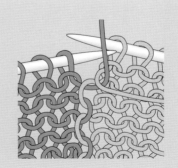

work button tabs as follows: *BO 3 sts at beg of next row, work first 3 sts in seed st and rem sts in St st. Work next 7 rows in St st with 3 sts of seed st for band. On next row, CO 3 sts and work 6 sts in seed st and rem sts in St st. Work next 7 rows in St st with 6 sts in seed st for band. Rep from * 6 more times (total of 7 tabs). After last tab, BO 3 sts and cont with 3 sts in seed st and St st to end. AT SAME TIME when piece measures 16", beg armhole shaping.

Shape armhole: BO 5 sts at armhole edge—44 (46, 48, 52, 54) sts. Cont in established patt until armhole measures 6", ending with WS row.

Shape neck: Put 27 (27, 27, 31, 31) sts on holder for neck opening. Dec 1 st at neck edge EOR 3 (3, 4, 4, 5) times—14 (16, 17, 17, 18) sts. Work until armhole measures same length as back. Put shoulder sts on holder.

SLEEVES

With smaller needles, CO 42 (42, 42, 44, 44) sts with MC. Work in seed st for 2". Change to larger needles and work in St st, inc 1 st at each edge on row 5 and then every 6 rows 11 (11, 11, 13, 13) times—66 (66, 66, 72, 72) sts. Work until sleeve measures 20" or desired length. BO all sts.

Work 2nd sleeve with CC.

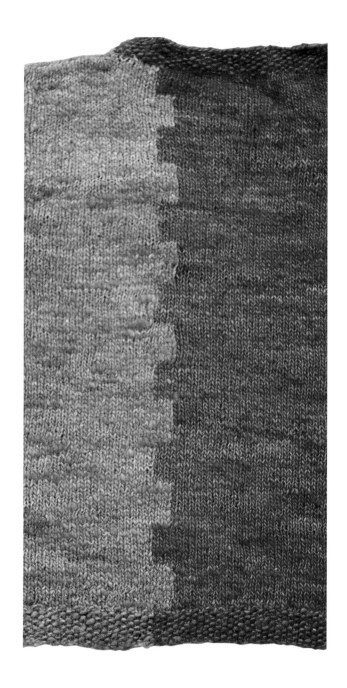

FINISHING

Block pieces lightly.

With right sides together, work 3-needle BO (see page 31) at each shoulder. Place right front on top of left front so that the right-front band overlaps the left-front band by 2 sts and sew in place with a whipstitch from the WS.

Neckband: With smaller 16" circular needle and MC, PU sts at front edge, front sts on holder, and back neck sts. Work in seed st for 1". BO all sts loosely.

Sew side seams of sweater. Sew sleeve seams. Sew in sleeves, matching MC and CC on each side. Sew buttons on tabs.

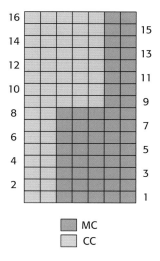

MC
CC

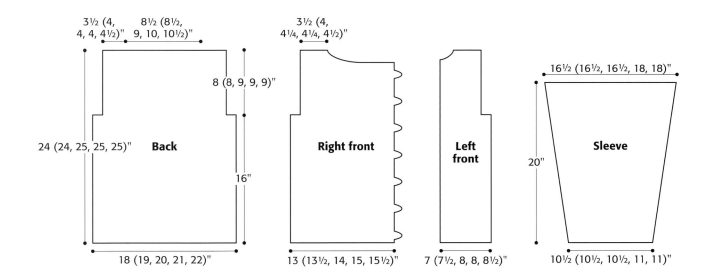

Side-to-Side Jacket

Side-to-Side Jacket

Knitting with a vibrant recycled silk-and-wool blend is an adventure worth trying. I wanted to play with lots of colors in this side-to-side jacket. On this coat of many colors, you too can experiment with how you want the color sequence to move. I picked my favorite skeins of colors and put them in front of me in a line, and I moved them around until I found a pleasing combination. Make a swatch or several swatches to see how the colors look when knit. The colors in a skein will have a different appearance when next to another color. Have fun with this project. Jump in and enjoy!

Skill level: Easy ◼◼☐☐

Sizes: Small (Medium, Large)
Finished bust: 36 (40, 46)"
Finished length: 24"

Size 8 circular needle, 32", or size to obtain gauge
Size 6 circular needle, 16"
Stitch holders
5 buttons, 1" diameter

MATERIALS

Himalaya Yarn (60% wool, 40% recycled silk; 100 g; 175 yds) (4)

MC	4 skeins	color 15 Teal
CC1	1 skein	color 141 Mustard
CC2	1 skein	color 150 Lime
CC3	1 skein	color 222 Aqua
CC4	1 skein	color 05 Magenta
CC5	1 skein	color 01 Red
CC6	1 skein	color 08 Purple
CC7	1 skein	color 07 Royal

GAUGE

16 sts and 22 rows = 4" in St st on larger needle

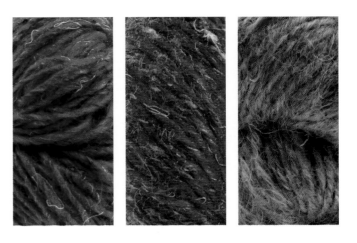

RIGHT SLEEVE

Jacket is knit side to side, beginning with right sleeve.
With larger needle and MC, CO 40 sts. *Do not
join into rnd.* Work 16 rows (or 8 ridges)
of garter st. Work in alternating stripes of 8
rows of a CC yarn in St st and 8 rows of MC
in garter st, and AT SAME TIME, inc 1 st at
each side every 6 rows 7 times and then inc
1 st at each side every 4 rows 8 times—70
sts. Cont until sleeve measures approx 18"
from beg.

BODY

CO 62 sts at beg of next 2 rows—194 sts.
Cont in alternating garter st and St st color
sequence as desired for 5 (6, 7½)".

BACK NECK

Work 97 sts and place rem sts on holder for
front. On back sts, cont in patt, dec 1 st at
neck edge once. Work back for 8". Add 1 st
at neck edge and put these sts on holder (to
be joined to front later).

RIGHT FRONT

Place front sts back onto needle. Work in established color sequence as for back. Dec 2 sts
at neck once, then 1 st EOR 6 times—89 sts.
When neck measures 3½", ending with a WS
row, make buttonhole band: Work 3 rows in
seed st. Place buttonholes, beg at neck edge
as follows: Work 10 sts in seed st, *BO 3 sts,
work 13 sts in seed st, rep from * 4 times
and work in seed st to end of row. On next
row, cont in seed st and CO 3 sts over BO
sts as required. Work 3 more rows in seed st.
BO all sts loosely.

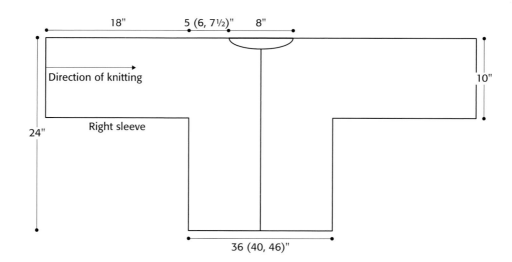

LEFT FRONT

CO 89 sts and work in seed st for 8 rows. Cont in established color sequence as for back, inc 1 st at neck EOR 6 times and then 2 sts once—97 sts.

JOIN FRONT TO BACK

PU back sts from holder and join front to back. Cont in patt for 5 (6, 7½)". BO 62 sts at beg of next 2 rows—70 sts rem for sleeve.

LEFT SLEEVE

Dec 1 st at each side every 4 rows 8 times, then 1 st every 6 rows 7 times—40 sts. When sleeve measures the same length as first sleeve and you have done 16 rows (or 8 ridges) of garter st, BO all sts.

FINISHING

Sew side seams and sleeve seams.

Neckband: With smaller needle, PU sts around neck opening. Work 2 rows in K1, P1 ribbing. Knit 4 rows. BO all sts.

Bottom band: With larger needle, PU sts along bottom edge of sweater and work 8 rows in garter st or K1, P1 ribbing. BO all sts.

Sew on buttons.

Textured Vest

Textured Vest

Designing with silk allows you to feel a yarn and then decide what to do with that experience. This one-of-a-kind merino and tussah silk hand-spun has the ability to be many things. I chose to make a textured vest using an earthy moss color with subtle shine. You can change where the buttons go to make it for a woman or a man. This is yet another garment I loved making because each stitch slid on the needles with grace.

Skill level: Intermediate ◀■■▢

Sizes: X-Small (Small, Medium, Large, X-Large)
Finished chest: 36 (40, 42, 44, 46)"
Finished length: 23 (25, 25, 26, 27)"

MATERIALS

6 (7, 7, 8, 8) skeins of Silk Tweed from
   Handspun on the Web (70% merino wool,
   30% tussah silk; 2.5 oz; 175 yds), color
   moss 🪢4
Size 6 circular needle, 36"
Size 8 circular needle, 36", or size to obtain
   gauge
Stitch holders
6 buttons, ¾" diameter

GAUGE

18 sts and 22 rows = 4" in patt st on larger
   needles

RIDGED RIB PATTERN

Worked in the rnd
(Multiple of 2 + 1)
Rnds 1 and 2: Knit.
Rnd 3 (RS): P1, *K1, P1, rep from * to end.
Rnd 4: K1, *P1, K1, rep from * to end.
Rep rnds 1–4 for patt.

RIDGED RIB PATTERN

Worked back and forth
(Multiple of 2 + 1)
Row 1 (RS): Knit.
Row 2: Purl.
Rows 3 and 4: P1, *K1, P1, rep from * to end.
Rep rows 1–4 for patt.

BODY

Vest is knit in the round up to the armholes, and then worked back and forth.

With smaller needles, CO 163 (181, 189, 199, 207) sts. Work 3 rows in P1, K1 ribbing. Make first buttonhole: Work 3 sts, BO 2 sts, and work to end of row. On next row, knit to last 5 sts, CO 2 sts over BO sts, and finish row. Work P1, K1 ribbing for 2". Put first and last 6 sts on a holder for front bands to be worked later—151 (169, 177, 187, 195) sts. Change to larger needles, beg ridged rib patt in the rnd, and cont until piece measures 14 (15, 15, 15, 16)" or desired length to underarm.

Divide for front and back: Work 32 (35, 38, 40, 44) sts, BO 9 sts for underarm, finish row. On next row, work 32 (35, 38, 40, 44) sts, BO 9 sts for underarm. Put front sts on holders.

BACK

Work 69 (81, 83, 89, 89) sts back and forth in ridged rib patt, dec 1 st at each armhole edge EOR 2 times—65 (77, 79, 85, 85) sts. Cont in established patt until armholes measure 9 (10, 10, 11, 11)" or desired length. Put 20 (22, 24, 26, 26) sts on holder for shoulder, BO 25 (33, 31, 33, 33) sts for back neck, and put rem 20 (22, 24, 26, 26) sts on holder.

FRONTS

PU front sts from holder. Working back and forth in established patt, dec 1 st at armhole edge EOR 2 times and AT SAME TIME, start neck shaping by dec 1 st at each neck edge every 3 rows until you have 20 (22, 24, 26, 26) sts. Work even until fronts measure same length as back.

FINISHING

Work 3-needle BO (see page 31) at shoulders.

Right-front button band: With smaller needles, PU 6 sts from holder and work K1, P1 ribbing up front band, joining band and vest by slipping last st from vest and placing it on left needle, then working vest st and next band st as one to join seam. Cont around neck until you reach the center st on back neck. Put these 6 sts on holder. Place 6 buttons evenly on button band.

Left-front buttonhole band: Work as for button band, making a buttonhole opposite every button (5 more) as follows: BO 2 sts for each buttonhole and then CO 2 sts over the bound-off sts on next row. When you reach back center, work 3-needle BO on all sts.

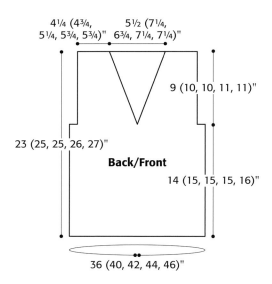

4¼ (4¾, 5¼, 5¾, 5¾)"   5½ (7¼, 6¾, 7¼, 7¼)"

9 (10, 10, 11, 11)"

23 (25, 25, 26, 27)"

Back/Front

14 (15, 15, 15, 16)"

36 (40, 42, 44, 46)"

Beaded Shrug

Beaded Shrug

At Stitches East, my eyes turned to Laura Glazier when I saw her wearing a beautiful shrug she designed and knit. I asked if she wanted to make one for this book and she said yes. So we picked out skeins of tsunmugi silk and some fabulous beads and Laura began knitting it immediately. This project will give you many hours of satisfying knitting pleasure—a showstopper for sure and a way to dress up for any formal occasion.

Skill level: Experienced ◖■■◗

One size: Large
Finished measurement from cuff to cuff: 56"
Back length from neck: 36"

MATERIALS

A   12 skeins of Item A-111 1/0.9 from Habu Textiles (100% silk; 28 g; 78 yds), color HA1 🔘

B   1 skein of Item A-1 2/17 from Habu Textiles (100% silk; 50 g; 450 yds), color 34 🔘

Size 5 circular needle, 29", or size to obtain gauge

3 large tubes of Caravan seed beads, size 8, color 650 grey

2 large tubes of Shiney brand black seed beads, size 8

2 large tubes of Swarovski black diamond crystals, 4 mm

2 large tubes of Shiney brand black teardrops, 4 mm

1 spool of Silamide beading thread

Size 10 beading needle
Tapestry needle
Size C-2 (2.75 mm) crochet hook
Stitch markers

GAUGE

20 sts and 32 rows = 4" in patterns 1, 2, and 3

PATTERN 1

Ridged Ribbon Eyelet
(Over odd number of sts)
Row 1 (RS): Knit.
Row 2: Purl.
Rows 3 and 4: Knit.
Row 5: *K2tog, YO, rep from *, end K1.
Row 6: Knit (and slide designated number of beads).

PATTERN 2

Hourglass Eyelet Pattern

(Multiple of 6 + 1)

Row 1 (RS): K6, *P1, K5, rep from *, end K1.

Row 2: K1, *P5, K1, rep from *.

Row 3: K1, *YO, ssk, P1, K2tog, YO, K1, rep from *.

Row 4: K1, P2, *K1, P5, rep from * to last 4 sts, K1, P2, K1.

Row 5: K3, *P1, K5, rep from * to last 4 sts, P1, K3.

Row 6: Rep row 4.

Row 7: K1, *K2tog, YO, K1, YO, ssk, P1, rep from *, end last rep K1 instead of P1.

Row 8: Rep row 2.

PATTERN 3

Reverse Ridged Ribbon Eyelet

(Over odd number of sts)

Row 1 (RS): Purl (and slide designated number of beads).

Row 2: *P2tog, YO, rep from * to last st, P1.

Rows 3 and 4: Purl.

Row 5: Knit.

Row 6: Purl.

DIRECTIONS

Shrug is worked from cuff to cuff.

String 50 black seed beads onto A.

With A, CO 1 st for selvage, CO 51 sts, sliding a bead between each st, CO 1 st for selvage— 53 sts. Knit selvage st at each end on rows 1–70 and rows 369–438. These selvage sts are not included in end st numbers. Only number of patt sts are given on rows 1–70 and rows 369–438.

Rows 1–7: K1, work in patt 1, K1.

Row 8: K1, cont in patt 1, inc 22 sts evenly across row, K1—73 patt sts.

Rows 9–12: K1, cont in patt 1, K1.

Rows 13–20: K1, work in patt 2, K1.

Row 21: K1, work in patt 1, K1.

Row 22: K1, cont in patt 1, inc 36 sts evenly across row, K1—109 patt sts.

Rows 23–26: K1, cont in patt 1, K1.

Rows 27–42: K1, work in patt 2, K1.

Row 43: K1, work in patt 1, K1.

Row 44: K1, cont in patt 1, inc 54 sts evenly across row, K1—163 patt sts.

Rows 45–48: K1, cont in patt 1, K1.

Rows 49–64: K1, work in patt 2, K1.

Row 65: K1, work in patt 1, K1.

Row 66: K1, cont in patt 1, inc 22 sts evenly across row, K1—185 patt sts.

Rows 67–70: K1, cont in patt 1, K1; pm on each end on row 70.

Row 71: Convert selvage st into patt st and work in patt 2.

Rows 72–94: Cont in patt 2.

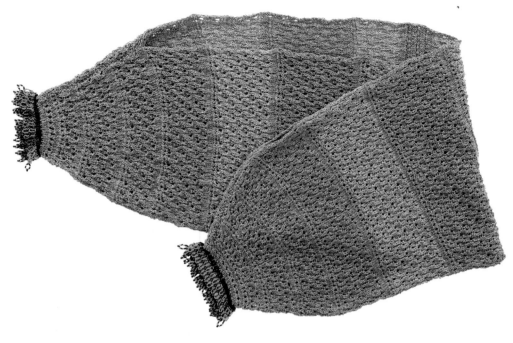

Rows 95–100: Work in patt 1.

Rows 101–132: Change to B and work in patt 2.

Rows 133–138: Change to A and work in patt 1.

Rows 139–178: Work in patt 2.

Rows 179–184: Work in patt 1.

Rows 185–208: Change to B and work in patt 2.

Rows 209–213: Change to A and work in patt 1.

Row 214: Cut yarn, string 93 black seed beads and reattach yarn. K2, (slide a bead, K2) 93 times, K1.

Rows 215–219: Cont in patt 1.

Row 220: Cut yarn, string 186 black seed beads and reattach yarn. K1, (slide a bead, K1) 186 times.

Rows 221–225: Cont in patt 1.

Row 226: Cut yarn, string 93 black seed beads and reattach yarn. K2, (slide a bead, K2) 93 times, K1.

Row 227: Purl.

Row 228: Purl.

Row 229: Knit.

Row 230: Purl.

Rows 231–254: Change to B and work in patt 2.

Rows 255–260: Change to A and work in patt 3.

Rows 261–300: Work in patt 2.

Rows 301–306: Work in patt 3.

Rows 307–338: Change to B and work in patt 2.

Rows 339–344: Change to A and work in patt 3.

Rows 345–368: Work in patt 2.

Row 369: Convert first and last st to single selvage as follows: K1, work in patt 3, K1; pm at beg and end of row.

Rows 370–372: K1, cont in patt 3, K1.

Row 373: K1, cont in patt 3, dec 22 sts evenly across row, K1—163 patt sts.

Row 374: K1, cont in patt 3, K1.

Rows 375–390: K1, work in patt 2, K1.

Rows 391–394: K1, work in patt 3, K1.

Row 395: K1, cont in patt 3, dec 54 sts evenly across row, K1—109 patt sts.

Row 396: K1, cont in patt 3, K1.

Rows 397–412: K1, work in patt 2, K1.

Rows 413–416: K1, work in patt 3, K1.

Row 417: K1, cont in patt 3, dec 36 sts evenly across row, K1—73 patt sts.

Row 418: K1, cont in patt 3, K1.

Rows 419–426: K1, work in patt 2, K1.

Rows 427–430: K1, work in patt 3, K1.

Row 431: K1, work in patt 1, dec 22 sts evenly across row, K1—51 patt sts.

Rows 432–438: K1, cont in patt 3, K1.

Row 439: Cut yarn and string 50 black seed beads onto yarn. BO pw, sliding a bead between each bound-off st.

FINISHING

Sew each sleeve from cuff edge to markers between selvage st and first st on each side of sleeve. Now cuffs are ready to be beaded (directions follow). Using crochet hook, work 1 row of sc around edges from marker to marker.

BEADED CUFF

Row 1: Using a double strand of beading thread, go through the first black bead on the cuff edge and string the following sequence: 5 black beads, 3 grey beads, and 5 black beads and then go through the next 2 black beads on the cuff edge. Rep sequence for entire row and go through last bead on cuff edge, first bead of cuff edge, and down first 5 black beads and 3 grey beads of first beaded net. Now slide 1 black bead, 1 crystal bead, and 1 black bead, then bead through the 3 grey beads of next beaded net. Cont the sequence of beading through the grey beads of next net and sliding 1 black bead, 1 crystal bead, and 1 black bead for entire row.

Row 2: Bead through the first set of 1 black bead, 1 crystal bead, and 1 black bead, then string 13 grey beads. Cont for entire row. Now bead through the first black bead, grey bead, black bead, and first 8 grey beads of first grey bead net and string 1 black bead, 1 crystal bead, and 1 black bead. For rest of row, bead through center 3 grey beads and string 1 black bead, 1 crystal bead, and 1 black bead; cont for entire row.

Row 3: Bead through first set of 1 black bead, 1 crystal bead, 1 black bead, then string 13 grey beads. Cont for entire row. Now bead through first 8 grey bead net and string 1 black bead, 1 crystal bead, and 1 black bead. For rest of row, bead through center 3 grey beads and string 1 black bead, 1 crystal bead, and 1 black bead.

Row 4: Bead through last 3 grey beads and 1 black bead, and string the following sequence: 3 black beads, 1 crystal bead, 2 black beads, 1 black teardrop, 2 black beads, 1 crystal bead, and 3 black beads; bead through 1 black bead, 3 grey beads, and 1 black bead; cont for entire row.

Rep rows 1–4 on second cuff.

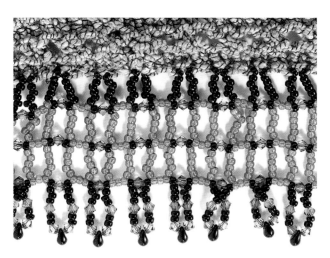

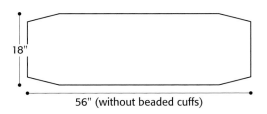

18"

56" (without beaded cuffs)

Poncho

Poncho

A poncho can be a fun way to try out new yarns, a combination of textures, and your own personal color choices. I used several kinds of yarn in this poncho to add some interest to it while knitting in a big circle. You can't go wrong when knitting this. I get so many compliments when wearing this simply made project.

Skill level: Beginner ◼☐☐▷

Sizes: Small (Medium, Large)
Bottom circumference: 72½ (76¼, 80)"
Finished length: 24 (28, 30)"

MATERIALS

Kathmandu from Queensland Collection (85% merino wool, 10% silk, 5% cashmere; 50 g; 104 yds) 🔠4

   MC   6 (7, 9) skeins   color 124
   CC   2 (2, 3) skeins   color 127

3 skeins of Mohair Kiss Ombre from Cascade Yarns (73% mohair, 22% wool, 5% nylon; 50 g; 98 yds), color 23063 🔠3

1 skein of Firenze Bouclé from Plymouth Yarn Company (30% wool, 30% acrylic, 40% nylon; 50 g; 47 yds), color 417 🔠4

Size 8 circular needles, 24" and 36", or size to obtain gauge

Stitch markers

GAUGE

16 sts and 18 rows = 4" in St st

DIRECTIONS

Poncho is worked from the neck down.

With 24" needle and bouclé, CO 70 (75, 80) sts. Join into rnd, being careful not to twist sts and pm at beg of rnd. Change to 2 strands of Ombre and work in K1, P1 ribbing for 5". On last rnd of ribbing, pm after every 14 (15, 16) sts. Use different-color marker to indicate beg of rnd.

Change to MC and 36" needle, beg St st and inc as follows:

Rnd 1: *K1f&b, knit to last st before marker, K1f&b, slm, rep from * 4 times—80 (85, 90) sts.

Rnd 2: Knit.

Work rnds 1 and 2 another 21 (22, 23) times—290 (305, 320 sts).

Work even until piece measures 21 (23, 24)". Add CC and work as follows: *K1 with CC, sl 1 MC, rep from * to end of rnd. Cont with CC in St st for 2 (3, 4)". Change to 1 strand each of Ombre and CC held tog, and work 4 rnds of garter st. Change to 2 strands of Ombre and work in garter st until piece measures 26 (28, 30)" or desired length. Work 2 rnds in garter st with bouclé. BO all sts. Block if necessary.

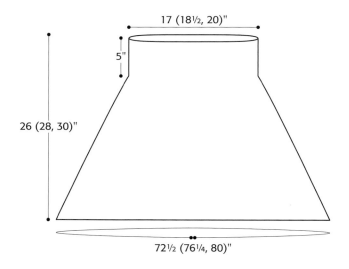

17 (18½, 20)"

5"

26 (28, 30)"

72½ (76¼, 80)"

Houndstooth Pullover

Houndstooth Pullover

Soft as butter, this silk-alpaca blend makes up beautifully in a two-color houndstooth pattern stitch. The vibrant colors play off one another and are perfect as a winter project. The yarn glides nicely on the needles, and the colors together bring out the beauty of dyed silk. This sweater was designed and knit by Aloisia Pollock.

Skill level: Intermediate ◼◼◼◻

Sizes: Small (Medium, Large, X-Large)
Finished bust: 38½ (40½, 42¾, 44¾)"
Finished length: 22 (22, 25, 26)"

MATERIALS

Alpaca Silk DK from Debbie Bliss (80% baby alpaca, 20% silk; 50 g; 105 m) 🧶3
  A 6 (7, 7, 8) skeins   color 26005
  B 6 (7, 7, 8) skeins   color 26007
Size 4 circular needle, 29"
Size 6 dpn or size to obtain gauge
Size 6 circular needles, 16" and 29", or size to obtain gauge
Stitch holders
Stitch markers

GAUGE

23 sts and 20 rows = 4" on larger needles

HOUNDSTOOTH PATTERN

(Multiple of 3)
Rnd 1: With A, K1, *sl 1 wyib, K2, rep from * to last 2 sts, sl 1 wyib, K1.
Rnd 2: Knit.
Rnd 3: With B, *sl 1 wyib, K2, rep from * to end.
Rnd 4: Knit.
Rep rnds 1–4 for patt.

BODY

Sweater is worked in the round up to the armholes, and then worked back and forth.
With smaller needles and A, CO 208 (220, 232, 244) sts. Join into rnd, pm at beg of rnd. K1 with A, P1 with B for 3". Change to larger needles and with A, inc 14 sts evenly across rnd—222 (234, 246, 258) sts.
Work in houndstooth patt until piece measures 13 (13, 15, 15)" from beg, ending with rnd 4.

DIVIDE FOR FRONT AND BACK

Back: Work 111 (117, 123, 129) sts and put on holder for front.

On back sts, work back and forth in houndstooth patt as established, working rows 1 and 3 as on page 74 and purling rows 2 and 4. K1f&b at beg of next 2 rows—113 (119, 125, 131) sts. Knit selvage st on rows 1 and 3 and purl selvage st on rows 2 and 4. Cont until back measures 17 (17, 18, 18)" from beg.

Shape neck: Work 39 (40, 42, 44) sts in patt, place 35 (39, 41, 43) sts on holder for neck, work 39 (40, 42, 44) sts in patt. Working both sides separately with separate balls of yarn, BO 1 st at each neck edge EOR 8 times—31 (32, 34, 36) sts for each shoulder. Work in patt until armhole measures 9 (9, 10, 11)". BO all sts.

Front: Work front same as back, but start neck shaping when armhole measures 15 (15, 17, 17)". Work same as on back.

SLEEVES (MAKE 2)

With dpn and A, CO 54 (56, 60, 60) sts. Join into rnd and pm. (K1 with A, P1 with B) across each row for 2". Change to larger 16" circular needles and inc 0 (1, 0, 0) st at beg of rnd. Work in houndstooth patt,

k1f&b at beg of rnd and k1f&b at end of rnd before marker every 6 rnds 10 times—74 (77, 80, 80) sts. Change to 29" circular needle when necessary to accommodate sts. Cont in patt and inc sts every 8 rnds until there are 104 (104, 116, 126) sts on needle. Work until sleeve measures 18 (19, 19, 20)" from beg. BO all sts.

FINISHING

Block pieces lightly. Sew shoulder seams.

Neckband: With 16" circular needle and A, PU sts around neck and work ribbing for 3" as follows: K1 with A, P1 with B. BO all sts loosely in A. Fold neckband in half toward inside and sew in place.

Sew in sleeves.

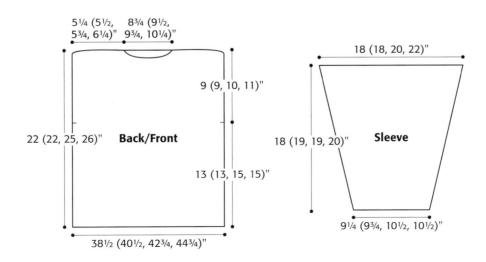

5¼ (5½, 5¾, 6¼)"   8¾ (9½, 9¾, 10¼)"

9 (9, 10, 11)"

22 (22, 25, 26)"   **Back/Front**

13 (13, 15, 15)"

38½ (40½, 42¾, 44¾)"

18 (18, 20, 22)"

18 (19, 19, 20)"   **Sleeve**

9¼ (9¾, 10½, 10½)"

Oversized Cardigan

Oversized Cardigan

After making several swatches for this oversized cardigan, I decided to introduce a new yarn from La Patrona, a hand-spun, linen-silk blend that I plied with silk tweed. The effect is dramatic—the look of hand-spun and hand-dyed yarn from Uruguay and finer silk tweed from Norway. I love the way this combination knits up. Since the project is large and takes a lot of yarn, I wanted to make sure it wouldn't lose its shape when worn, a casualty of some silk garments.

Generally, buttons on women's sweaters are on the left. With this sweater, they're on the right because I got so caught up knitting these wonderful yarns that I didn't realize where I was putting the buttonholes. Directions are written for buttons on the left.

Skill level: Easy ◖■□□

Sizes: Small (Medium, Large)
Finished bust: 39 (50, 60)"
Finished length: 23"

MATERIALS

6 (7, 8) skeins of Judith from La Patrona (85% linen, 15% silk; 4.5 oz; 200 yds), color 8 (3)

6 (7, 8) skeins of Silke-Tweed from Garnstudio (52% silk, 48% lamb's wool; 50 g; 200 m), color 9 (3)

Size 6 needles

Size 9 needles or size to obtain gauge
Stitch holders
6 glass buttons from Shipyard Point Glassworks, ⅝" diameter

GAUGE

14 sts and 20 rows = 4" in St st on larger needles with 1 strand each of Judith and Silke-Tweed held tog

NOTE:
Use 1 strand of Judith and 1 strand of Silke-Tweed held together throughout project.

BACK

With larger needles, CO 70 (90, 110) sts. Work in St st for 14".

Shape armholes: BO 6 sts at beg of next 2 rows—58 (78, 98) sts. Work even until armhole measures 9", ending with WS row.

Shape shoulders: K18 (24, 29) sts and put these on stitch holder, knit to end of row. On next row, P18 (24, 29) sts and put these on holder.

Collar: Cont in St st on rem 22 (30, 40) sts for 4". BO all sts loosely.

LEFT FRONT

With larger needles, CO 36 (46, 54) sts. Work in St st for 14", ending with WS row.

Shape armhole: BO 6 sts at armhole edge, knit to end—30 (40, 48) sts. Cont in St st until armhole measures 9", ending with RS row.

Shape shoulder and collar: Work 12 (16, 19) sts for collar and put rem 18 (24, 29) sts on holder for shoulder.

Collar: Cont in St st on 12 (16, 19) sts for 4". BO all sts loosely.

RIGHT FRONT

With larger needles, CO 36 (46, 54) sts. Work in St st for 3", ending with WS row.

Make first buttonhole: Knit to last 4 sts, YO 2 times, K4. On next row, P4, drop both YOs, purl to end of row. Cont in St st, making buttonhole every 3" (or 14 rows) 5 more times (total of 6 buttonholes) and AT SAME TIME shape armhole when front measures 14", ending with RS row.

Shape armhole: BO 6 sts at armhole edge—30 (40, 48) sts. Work even until armhole measures 9", making rem buttonholes. End with WS row.

Shape shoulder and collar: Work 18 (24, 29) sts and put these on holder for shoulder.

Collar: Cont in St st on 12 (16, 19) sts for 4". BO all sts loosely.

SLEEVES (MAKE 2)

With smaller needles, CO 58 sts. Work in St st for 1". Change to larger needles and cont in St st, inc 1 st at each edge every 10 rows 3 times—64 sts. Work even until sleeve measures 15". BO all sts.

POCKETS (MAKE 2)

With larger needles, CO 22 sts. Work in St st for 6", ending with a RS row. Knit 1 row. BO all sts.

FINISHING

Work 3-needle BO (see page 31) to join back and front at shoulders. Sew side seams. Sew sleeve seams. Sew in sleeves, making sure seams are aligned at bottom of armhole. Sew front collar to back collar along seam on each side of sweater.

Place pockets 5" from front bands and along bottom edge of garment. Make sure sts on pocket are lined up with sts on garment. Sew sides and bottom of pocket, using a whip-stitch.

Sew on buttons opposite buttonholes.

At bottom of each sleeve seam, fold RS tog for 1" and sew up seam for 1", making a small tuck. Tack seam to side of sleeve.

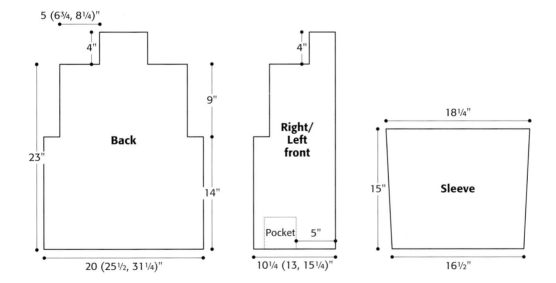

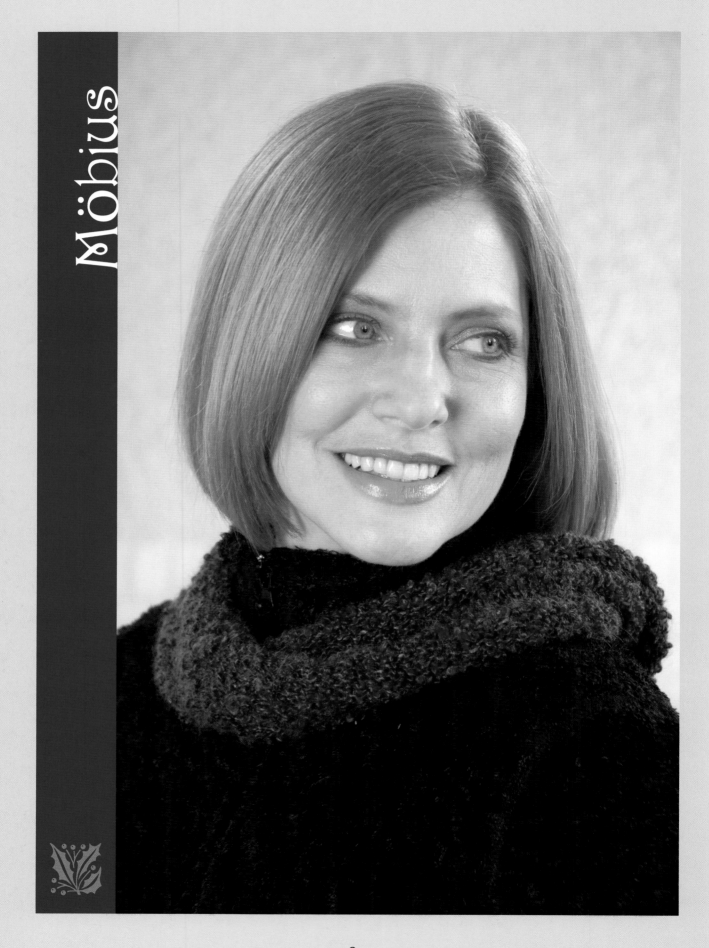

Möbius

Möbius

Making a Möbius is like making mittens, a necessity for the Maine winters. This time I picked out some of my hand-dyed silk bouclé and put the yarn to work. Simple and functional, warm and easy to wear, this Möbius takes no time to knit. A great present for people you love—just keep changing the color to fit each personality.

Skill level: Beginner ◼☐☐◻

One size: 8" wide x 30" circumference

MATERIALS

1 skein of Silk Bouclé from Pine Tree Yarns (42% mohair, 25% silk, 25% wool, 8% nylon; 4 oz; 200 yds), color sapphire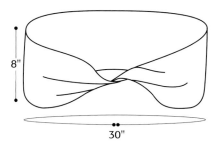
Size 10½ circular needle, 16", or size to obtain gauge
Stitch marker

GAUGE

14 sts and 18 rows = 4" in patt

DIRECTIONS

CO 105 sts. Twist sts and join into rnd, pm. Work in St st (knit every rnd) until piece measures 8" or desired width. BO all sts loosely.

Frost Flowers Shawl (1)

Frost Flowers Shawl

Anne Dill designed and knit this incredible shawl using a natural two-ply tussah silk.

The sheen of the silk and the delicate pattern give this shawl an exquisite appearance.

Anne made a second shawl using single-ply silk and smaller needles. While both shawls

have the same number of rows, the two-ply shawl was blocked to a 33" length, and the

single-ply shawl was left unblocked, producing a completely different light texture.

Skill level: Expert ◀■■▶

Sizes:
Shawl 1: Approx 33" long (fully blocked)
Shawl 2: Approx 26" long (unblocked)

MATERIALS FOR SHAWL 1

5 skeins of Rapunzel 2-ply from Henry's Attic
(100% tussah silk; 5.2 oz; 322 yds), color
Tussah (❨3❩)
Size 10 circular needle, 36", or size to obtain
gauge
Size E-4 (3.5 mm) crochet hook
Stitch markers

MATERIALS FOR SHAWL 2

3 skeins of Rapunzel 1-ply from Henry's Attic
(100% tussah silk; 3.5 oz; 437 yds), color
Tussah (❨1❩)
Size 6 circular needle, 36"
Size 7 circular needle, 36", or size to obtain
gauge
Size D-3 (3.25 mm) crochet hook

GAUGE

Shawl 1: 18 sts and 24 rows = 4" on size
10 needles
Shawl 2: 28 sts and 34 rows = 4" on size
7 needles

CHART

Read odd-numbered rows from right to left,
and even-numbered rows from left to right.

DIRECTIONS

*Although this shawl makes a full circle when blocked,
it's not knit in the round. It is knit back and forth
from the neck down. The shawl is made up of nine
lace-diamond, wedge-shaped sections separated by
10 frost-flower panels. A one-stitch seed-stitch border
separates each section and panel, and a three-stitch
seed-stitch border is used for the first and last three
stitches of every row.*

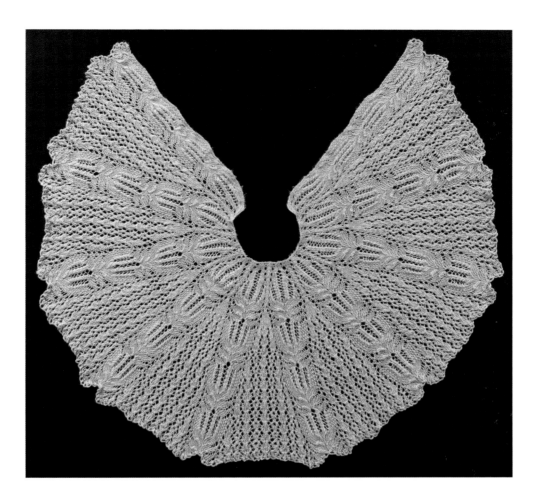

Shawl 1: Use size 10 circular needle and 2-ply Rapunzel tussah silk.

Shawl 2: Use size 6 circular needle and 1-ply Rapunzel tussah silk for rows 1–62, and size 7 circular needle for rows 63–110.

CO 53 sts and beg chart.

On each row, work 3-st seed-st border, then work (frost-flower panel, 1-st seed-st border, lace-diamond wedge-shaped section, 1-st seed-st border) 9 times. To help keep track of each patt within the repeats, pm between each section of rep. End with frost-flower panel, followed by 3-st seed-st border.

FINISHING

With crochet hook, sc into first 2 sts on needles, ch 6, sc into next 2 sts on needles, ch 6, and so on to end of row. Weave in ends.

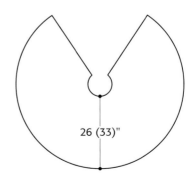

26 (33)"

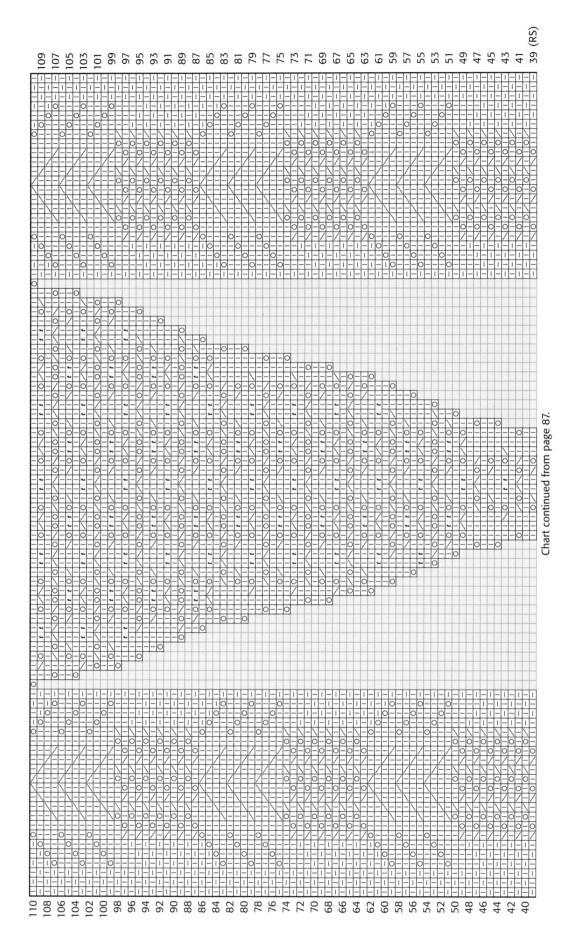

Chart continued from page 87.

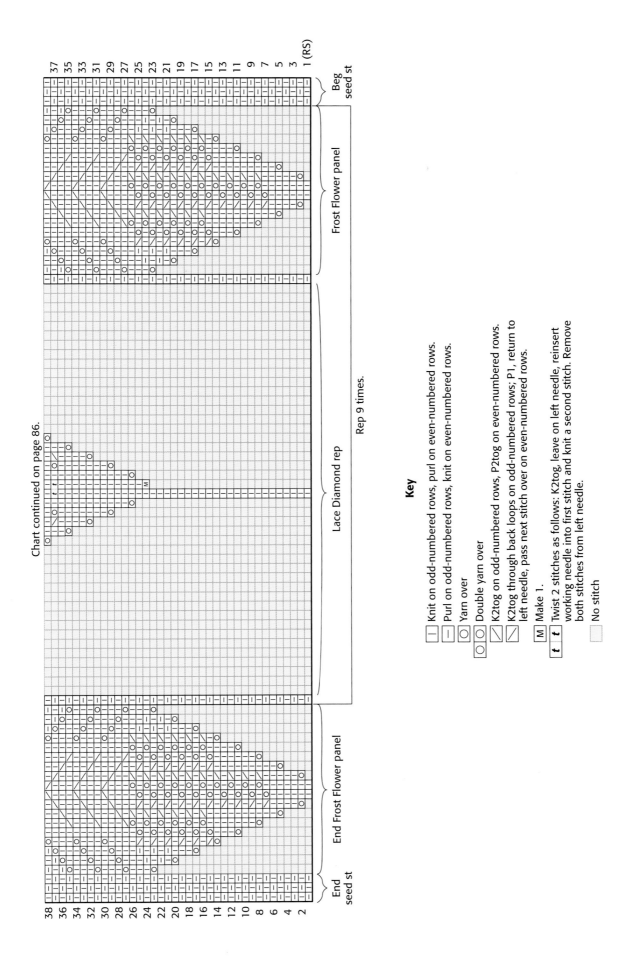

Chart continued on page 86.

Rep 9 times.

37 35 33 31 29 27 25 23 21 19 17 15 13 11 9 7 5 3 1 (RS)

Beg seed st

Frost Flower panel

Lace Diamond rep

38 36 34 32 30 28 26 24 22 20 18 16 14 12 10 8 6 4 2

End seed st

End Frost Flower panel

Key

| Knit on odd-numbered rows, purl on even-numbered rows.

− Purl on odd-numbered rows, knit on even-numbered rows.

○ Yarn over

○○ Double yarn over

\ K2tog on odd-numbered rows, P2tog on even-numbered rows.

/ K2tog through back loops on odd-numbered rows; P1, return to left needle, pass next stitch over on even-numbered rows.

M Make 1.

t Twist 2 stitches as follows: K2tog, leave on left needle, reinsert working needle into first stitch and knit a second stitch. Remove both stitches from left needle.

No stitch

87

Scarf and Hat

Scarf and Hat

Two exquisite yarns, a silk bouclé and a one-ply silk, are incredible to knit with. I wanted a textured look that would show off the individual yarns while finding unity with each other. After several swatches, I came up with this scarf pattern, which keeps both yarns on the needle and carries them up the side separately. This scarf knits up quickly, and you can easily experience why silk feels so good in the hands.

Skill level:
Scarf: Beginner ◖☐☐▢
Hat: Easy ◖▩☐▢

One size
Scarf: 6" x 44"
Adult hat: 22" circumference

MATERIALS FOR SCARF

A 1 skein of Daisany from Jade Sapphire (100% silk bouclé; 55 g; 106 yds), color 38 Wasabi (3)
B 1 skein of Maju from Jade Sapphire (100% silk; 50 g; 85 yds), color 38 Wasabi (3)
Size 8 needles or size to obtain gauge

MATERIALS FOR HAT

A 1 skein of Daisany from Jade Sapphire, color 38 Wasabi
B 1 skein of Maju from Jade Sapphire, color 38 Wasabi

Size 6 dpn and 16" circular needle or size to obtain gauge
Stitch marker

GAUGE

Scarf: 14 sts and 20 rows = 4"
Hat: 16 sts and 22 rows = 4"

SEED STITCH

Row 1: *P1, K1, rep from * to end.
Row 2: Purl the knit sts and knit the purl sts as they face you.

SCARF DIRECTIONS

When changing yarns, carry yarns loosely up side.
With A, CO 3 sts and knit 2 rows. Change to B, inc 1 st at beg of row and work 2 rows in seed st. Cont to inc 1 st at beg of each row, and alternate 4 knit rows with A and 2 seed-st rows with B (working new sts into seed-st patt) until there are 24 sts on needle.

Cont to alternate yarns, knit 4 rows with A, then work 2 rows of seed st with B. Work until scarf is 38" from beg or desired length.

Cont to alternate yarns, dec 1 st at beg of each row until 3 sts rem, ending with 2 rows of A. BO 3 sts.

Tassels: cut 8 pieces, 12" long, of each yarn. Using 4 strands of each yarn per tassel, attach tassels on each end as you would add a fringe.

HAT DIRECTIONS

Earflaps are worked first, and then rest of hat.

Earflap (Make 2)

With A, CO 3 sts. Knit 2 rows.

Rows 1 and 2: With B, inc 1 st, work seed st to end of row.

Rows 3–6: With A, inc 1 st, knit to end of row.

Rep rows 1–6 until 23 sts are on needle, ending with row 2.

Cut yarns and keep sts on needle.

Make second earflap.

Hat

With A, knit across earflap, CO 24 sts, knit across second earflap, CO 18 sts—88 sts. Join into rnd and pm. *Work 4 rnds in garter st (knit 1 rnd, purl 1 rnd) with A, then 2 rnds in seed st with B, rep from * until hat measures 4" from CO. Purl 8 rnds with A.

Turn work around so WS is facing you. Make a folded seam as follows: Yarn is on left needle; with right needle, PU st from first st in rnd below st on needle and slip it to left needle, then knit these 2 sts tog. The st is now on right needle. Cont in this manner until all sts have been picked up and knit tog, forming a fold. At the seam, PU 2 more sts to make 90 sts total. Knit 1 rnd.

Beg dec rnds, changing to dpn when necessary.

Rnd 1: With A, (K8, K2tog) to end—81 sts.

Rnd 2: Knit.

Rnd 3: With A, (K7, K2tog) to end—72 sts.

Rnd 4: Knit.

Rnd 5: With B, (K6, K2tog) to end—63 sts.

Rnd 6: Knit.

Rnd 7: With A, (K5, K2tog) to end—54 sts.

Rnd 8: Knit.

Rnd 9: With A, (K4, K2tog) to end—45 sts.

Rnd 10: Knit.

Rnd 11: With B, (K3, K2tog) to end—36 sts.

Rnd 12: Knit.

Rnd 13: With A, (K2, K2tog) to end—27 sts.

Rnd 14: Knit.

Rnd 15: With A, (K1, K2tog) to end—18 sts.

Rnd 16: Knit.

Rnd 17: With B, (K2tog) to end—9 sts.

Rnd 18: Knit.

Cut a 5" tail and pull yarn tightly through rem sts and weave in tail.

Tassels: Cut 8 pieces, 12" long, from each yarn. Using 4 strands of each yarn per tassel, attach tassel to ends of earflaps as for a fringe.

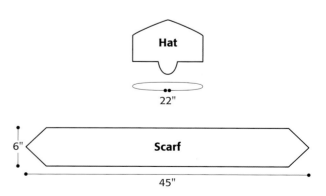

Abbreviations and Glossary

beg	begin(ning)
BO	bind off
CC	contrasting color
ch	chain
CO	cast on
cont	continue, continuing
dec	decrease(s), decreasing
dpn	double-pointed needle
EOR	every other row (round)
g	gram(s)
garter st	garter stitch (back and forth: knit every row; in the round: knit 1 round, purl 1 round)
inc	increase(s), increasing
K	knit
K1f&b	knit into front and back of same stitch (one-stitch increase)
K2tog	knit 2 stitches together (one-stitch decrease, right slant)
K2togtbl	knit 2 stitches together through back loops (one-stitch decrease, left slant)
kw	knitwise
m	meter(s)
M1	make 1 stitch (one-stitch increase)
MC	main color
oz	ounce(s)
P	purl
patt	pattern

pm	place marker
psso	pass slipped stitch over
P2sso	pass 2 slipped stitches over
P2tog	purl 2 stitches together (one-stitch decrease)
PU	pick up and knit (with right side facing unless otherwise indicated)
pw	purlwise
rem	remain(ing)
rep	repeat(s)
rnd(s)	round(s)
RS	right side
sc	single crochet
slm	slip marker
sl st	slip stitch
ssk	slip, slip, knit 2 stitches together (slip 2 stitches one at a time, insert left needle in front of right needle, and knit 2 stitches together; one stitch decrease, left slant)
st(s)	stitch(es)
St st	stockinette stitch (back and forth: knit on right side, purl on wrong side; in the round: knit every round)
tog	together
WS	wrong side
yds	yards
YO(s)	yarn over(s)

Useful Information

METRIC CONVERSIONS

Yards x .91 = meters   Grams x .035 = ounces

Meters x 1.09 = yards   Ounces x 28.35 = grams

SKILL LEVELS

■□□□ **Beginner:** Projects for first-time knitters using basic knit and purl stitches; minimal shaping.

■■□□ **Easy:** Projects using basic stitches, repetitive stitch patterns, and simple color changes; simple shaping and finishing.

■■■□ **Intermediate:** Projects using a variety of stitches, such as basic cables and lace, simple intarsia, and techniques for double-pointed needles and knitting in the round; midlevel shaping.

■■■■ **Experienced:** Projects using advanced techniques and stitches, such as short rows, Fair Isle, more intricate intarsia, cables, lace patterns, and numerous color changes.

YARN-WEIGHT SYMBOLS

YARN-WEIGHT SYMBOL AND CATEGORY NAMES	① Super Fine	② Fine	③ Light	④ Medium	⑤ Bulky	⑥ Super Bulky
TYPE OF YARNS IN CATEGORY	Sock, Fingering, Baby	Sport, Baby	DK, Light Worsted	Worsted, Afghan, Aran	Chunky, Craft, Rug	Bulky, Roving
KNIT GAUGE RANGES IN STOCKINETTE STITCH TO 4"	27 to 32 sts	23 to 26 sts	21 to 24 sts	16 to 20 sts	12 to 15 sts	6 to 11 sts
RECOMMENDED NEEDLE IN U.S. SIZE RANGE	1 to 3	3 to 5	5 to 7	7 to 9	9 to 11	11 and larger

Resources

Aurora Yarns
www.aurorayarns.com
Silke-Tweed

Cascade Yarns
www.cascadeyarns.com
Pima Silk, Bollicine Ischia Silk, Mohair Kiss Ombre

Classic Elite Yarns
www.classiceliteyarns.com
Classic Silk

The Fibre Company
www.TheFiberCo.com
Terra

Fiesta Yarns
www.fiestayarns.com
La Luz Multi

Habu Textiles
www.habutextiles.com
Item A-111, item A-1 2/17

Handspun on the Web
www.handspun-on-the-web.com
Hand-spun merino and silk

Henrys Attic, Inc.
5 Mercury Ave.
Monroe, NY 10950-5226
(845) 783-3930
Rapunzel 1-ply, Rapunzel 2-ply, Spun silk NM 4/2

Himalaya Yarn
www.HimalayaYarn.com
Tibet 60% wool, 40% recycled silk

Jade Sapphire
www.jadesapphire.com
Daisany, Maju

JHB International, Inc.
www.buttons.com
Assorted buttons

Knitting Fever
www.knittingfever.com
*Noro Silk Garden, Kathmandu Aran,
Debbie Bliss alpaca silk DK*

La Patrona
Mimi Brett
PO Box 767
Exeter, NH 03833
Judith

Pine Tree Yarns
www.pinetreeyarns.com
Silk bouclé

Plymouth Yarn Company
www.plymouthyarns.com
Firenze Bouclé

Shipyard Glassworks
PO Box 113
Franklin, ME 04634
(207) 565-2428
Glass buttons

Tilli Tomas
www.tillitomas.com
Silken Shimmer, Disco Lights

About the Designers

CARLA GIUFFRIDA

Carla Giuffrida of Eldred, New York, has always had a passion for fiber arts. Starting as a child sewing doll clothes, she then moved on to crocheting, knitting, weaving, spinning, and dyeing. She owned Coulter Studios in New York City years ago, one of the first yarn stores to specialize in natural fiber, imported yarns, and unique designer knitting patterns. Now she teaches fiber arts at the Homestead School in Glen Spey, New York, where she loves seeing the children enjoy knitting, spinning, and weaving. Her latest endeavor is starting the yarn department in a new shop, the Four Corners of Artful Living, in Narrowsburg, New York. She is the knitting instructor and buyer and is happy to be inspired by the beautiful yarns that fill the shop.

Email: 12732@yahoo.com

LAURA GLAZIER

Laura Glazier graduated from Moore College of Art with a bachelor's degree in Textile Design and Jewelry and received her master's in Textile Design from RIT School of American Craftsman. She has taught textile design at the Worcester Craft Center, the Peak Program in the Worcester School System, the Decordova Museum, and the YWCA in Boston.

In 1986 she started a custom-design jewelry business, and in 1993 she started to teach knitting and to custom design her own knit patterns. She designed a number of patterns for her students and then in 2001 began producing patterns for publication. She is now adding beads to her knit patterns, which combine the elements of jewelry with her knit designs.

Her beaded scarf design appeared in the Fall 2003 edition of *Vogue Knitting* magazine. The Spring 2005 edition of *Vogue Knitting* featured her Four Seasons Pillows, which also combine beading with knitting.

Laura lives in Worcester, Massachusetts, with her husband and two Cavalier King Charles spaniels, Isadora and Gabriella.

Email: artfulknitting@msn.com

ANNE E DILL

Known to her friends and colleagues as a computer wizard as well as a gourmet cook, Anne Dill has been designing textiles for many years. "As unorthodox as it may sound," she says, "I enjoy taking a line and turning it into a plane. I particularly enjoy taking a series of knit-togethers and holes and turning them into things of exquisite beauty."

The shawls presented here are both intended to enhance the form that wears them and showcase the silk used to create them. "Enjoy these patterns," Anne says, "and use them to make your world a more beautiful place."

Mailing address: 233 Federal St., Unit 7, Wiscasset, ME 04578

ALOISIA POLLOCK

Aloisia Pollock was born and raised in Austria, where knitting is as much a part of the culture and early childhood education as is music. Her first knitting project, at the age of four, was a pair of knee-length wool underpants knit in the round. These are a real toasty treat during the long winters in the Alps. Aloisia's second-grade teacher taught her how to design and knit

clothes for her doll. Later, she supplemented her high school and college allowances by knitting and crocheting sweaters and dresses for others.

Her ten-plus years in the New York City business world saw her knitting for relaxation and meditation. Christmas presents were started in June and consisted of knitted garments, crocheted curtains and tablecloths, and embroidered and cross-stitched wall hangings.

In 1988 Aloisia moved to Maine, and knitting took center stage again. She soon realized that her design style was very different from American knitwear. Her American friends knit and designed with an abundance of yarns and colors at their disposal. Aloisia had grown up amidst the scarcity of postwar Europe and had to design as a minimalist from whatever yarn was available— what she'd been given or what she was able to recycle from old and heavily worn sweaters.

Aloisia finds working with Elaine to be a treat, because Elaine's colorful hand-dyed yarns prompt the artist within into action. She also cherishes her collaboration with fiber producers, designing knitwear for her sheep-farmer and llama-farmer friends and exhibiting products and patterns at local fiber fairs.

Email: sunset@dialmaine.com

Knitting and Crochet Titles

Martingale® & COMPANY

America's Best-Loved Craft & Hobby Books®
America's Best-Loved Knitting Books®

CROCHET

Classic Crocheted Vests

Crochet for Babies and Toddlers

Crochet for Tots

Crochet from the Heart

Crocheted Aran Sweaters

Crocheted Lace

Crocheted Socks!

Crocheted Sweaters

The Essential Book of Crochet Techniques NEW!

Eye-Catching Crochet NEW!

First Crochet

Fun and Funky Crochet

The Little Box of Crocheted Hats and Scarves

The Little Box of Crocheted Ponchos and Wraps NEW!

More Crocheted Aran Sweaters

KNITTING

200 Knitted Blocks

365 Knitting Stitches a Year: Perpetual Calendar

Big Knitting

Blankets, Hats, and Booties NEW!

Dazzling Knits

Everyday Style NEW!

Fair Isle Sweaters Simplified

First Knits

Funky Chunky Knitted Accessories NEW!

Handknit Style

Knits for Children and Their Teddies

Knits from the Heart

Knitted Shawls, Stoles, and Scarves

The Knitter's Book of Finishing Techniques

Knitting with Hand-Dyed Yarns

Knitting with Novelty Yarns

Lavish Lace

The Little Box of Knitted Ponchos and Wraps

The Little Box of Knitted Throws

The Little Box of Scarves

The Little Box of Scarves II

The Little Box of Sweaters

Perfectly Brilliant Knits

The Pleasures of Knitting

Pursenalities

Pursenality Plus NEW!

Rainbow Knits for Kids

Ribbon Style NEW!

Sarah Dallas Knitting

Saturday Sweaters

Sensational Knitted Socks

Simply Beautiful Sweaters

A Treasury of Rowan Knits

The Ultimate Knitted Tee

The Yarn Stash Workbook NEW!

Our books are available at bookstores and your favorite craft, fabric, and yarn retailers. If you don't see the title you're looking for, visit us at **www.martingale-pub.com** or contact us at:

1-800-426-3126

International: 1-425-483-3313
Fax: 1-425-486-7596
Email: info@martingale-pub.com